CULTURE AND
ANARCHY IN
IRELAND
1890–1939

FOR IAN GREGOR

CULTURE AND ANARCHY IN IRELAND

1890–1939

BY

F. S. L. LYONS

THE FORD LECTURES DELIVERED
IN THE UNIVERSITY OF OXFORD IN
THE HILARY TERM OF 1978

Oxford   New York

OXFORD UNIVERSITY PRESS

Oxford University Press, Walton Street, Oxford OX2 6DP

Oxford New York Toronto
Delhi Bombay Calcutta Madras Karachi
Petaling Jaya Singapore Hong Kong Tokyo
Nairobi Dar es Salaam Cape Town
Melbourne Auckland

and associated companies in
Berlin Ibadan

First published by Oxford University Press 1979
First issued as an Oxford University Press paperback 1982
Reprinted 1989, 1991

British Library Cataloguing in Publication Data

Lyons, F. S. L.
Culture and anarchy in Ireland 1890–1939
1. Ireland—Politics and government—1837–1901
2. Ireland—Politics and government—20th century
3. Ireland—Civilization
I. Title
941.5082'1   DA957
ISBN 0–19–285121–7

Library of Congress Cataloging in Publication Data
Lyons, F. S. L. (Francis Stewart Leland), 1923–1983
Culture and anarchy in Ireland, 1890–1939 (Ford lectures; 1978) (Oxford paperbacks)
'The Ford lectures delivered in the University of Oxford in the
Hilary term of 1978' Includes bibliographical references and index
Contents: Unity and diversity—After Parnell—Irish Ireland
versus Anglo–Irish Ireland—etc.
1. Ireland—Politics and government—1837–1901
2. Ireland—Politics and government—20th century
3. Ireland—Civilization.   I. Title.   II. series
[DA957.L94 1982]   941.5081   82–6515   AACR2
ISBN 0–19–285121–7 (pbk.)

Printed in Great Britain

PREFACE

FOR any historian to be invited to deliver the Ford Lectures before the University of Oxford is a climactic moment in his career, but for an Irish historian the honour is quite literally a unique one. So far as I am aware, Ireland has not provided the theme for any previous series of lectures and I am deeply indebted to the electors for enabling me to break new ground by choosing a subject which, while not unconnected with English history, is yet intended primarily as a contribution to Irish history.

The Ford Lectures usually survey large matters in a small space and this series is no exception. The version printed here is essentially the same as, though slightly longer than, the one I delivered in Hilary term, 1978. The difference is largely accounted for by the reinsertion of material previously jettisoned by a lecturer obsessed by the ideal of finishing each lecture on the stroke of the appointed hour.

To attempt to deal in six lectures with the clash of cultures in modern Ireland is to be made acutely aware of how much work remains to be done in this contentious field. Indeed, it would be no exaggeration to say that the study of cultural history in any sense of the term is still in its infancy in my country. This book therefore makes no claim to be comprehensive or definitive and I shall be content if it comes to be regarded as a signpost pointing succeeding scholars in new directions.

A word should perhaps be said about the time-scale of these lectures. While I have deliberately concentrated attention on what I regard as the critical period between the fall of Parnell in 1890 and the death of Yeats in 1939, I have not felt constrained to remain absolutely within the limits imposed by those two dates. In the first lecture I have thought it desirable to give a brief sketch of the nineteenth century, and in dealing with Ulster, for reasons I have tried to make clear in the fifth lecture, I have ranged much further back in time, believing as I do that the long view is essential if we are to see the cultural tensions of that province in a true perspective. On the other hand, I found no difficulty in regarding 1939 as the end of an epoch in both parts of Ireland, though for different reasons. In the south the disappearance of Yeats from the scene was the culmination of a sequence of events which for a decade previously had been presaging the end of the Anglo-Irish culture of which he was the chief protagonist and the crowning glory. And in the north the onset of the Second World War and of the social revolution that followed it set in motion a complex transformation, cultural as well as political, of which we are only now beginning to see the extent and the consequences.

It is a very great pleasure to acknowledge the warmth and generosity of the hospitality I received in Oxford. I was made welcome by so many people that it is impossible to name all of them, but at the risk of being invidious I wish to record my particular thanks to Lord and Lady Blake, Professor H. R. Trevor-Roper, Professor Michael Howard, Lord Briggs, Dr Anne Whiteman, Professor Richard Ellmann, Mr Patrick Thompson, Dr John Kelly, the Reverend W. L. R. Watson, Mr D. M. Davin, and the late Eric Dodds to whom also, as the literary executor of Louis MacNeice, I am indebted for permission to quote the lines from the poet's works which appear on pp. 122-3. I am happy to pay tribute to the admirable efficiency with which Miss Geraldine Yeats made all the arrangements for my visits to Oxford. But most of all I am grateful to the Provost of Oriel College, and to his sister Miss Mary Turpin, for making Oriel a second home for me and for their great kindness to my wife and myself.

I wish, finally, to record my deepest thanks to those who helped me in various ways with the preparation of these lectures—to Mr David White, Miss Aileen Campbell, Miss Daphne Gill, Miss Frances Gwynn, and especially Miss Ann Sheil for her unerring ability to produce an immaculate typescript from the most unpromising materials. As always, my ultimate debt is to my wife who on this occasion shared my travels as well as my travails.

The Provost's House,   F. S. L. Lyons
Trinity College, Dublin

CONTENTS

I

Unity and Diversity

IN the second act of *The Importance of Being Earnest* that admirable governess, Miss Prism, has occasion to instruct her charge, Cecily Cardew. 'Cecily, you will read your political economy in my absence. The chapter on the fall of the rupee you may omit. It is somewhat too sensational.' On the same principle of selection, the delicately nurtured reader ought not to be exposed to a large part of the modern history of Oscar Wilde's country. For, despite the fact that the generation of historians to which I have the honour to belong has laboured with exemplary sobriety to bring the subject within the bounds of academic decorum, sensationalism keeps breaking in.

This, though apparently unavoidable—and the biographer of Parnell, for one, cannot claim to have avoided it—has had a deplorable effect both upon the study of the history of Ireland and upon the attitude of an ill-informed public towards that study. Because with us the sensational has become almost commonplace, it has been too easy to analyse the Irish question not just in political terms but in terms of the politics of violence. We in Ireland are all in a sense children of the revolution—more precisely, of the revolutionary decade 1912 to 1922—and for the pasty sixty years scholars and statesmen alike seem to have been mesmerized by the Easter Rising of 1916. It is hardly surprising, therefore, that those responsible for government, on either side of the Irish Sea, should have been almost wholly preoccupied with trying to find political solutions for problems which in reality are much more complex. Political solutions are indeed urgently needed, but they will continue to be as unavailing in the future as in the past if they go on ignoring the essence of the Irish situation, which is the collision of a variety of cultures within an island whose very smallness makes their juxtaposition potentially, and often actually, lethal. Recent events in Northern Ireland have certainly shown us that two very different communities are at death-grips with each other, but the fact that this conflict is so often described in religious terms has still further confounded confusion, leaving many observers convinced that a people so inveterately addicted to its ancient, obscure quarrels is best left to its own murderous devices.

Yet it would be a tragic turn of fate if the Irish were to be abandoned to possible self-annihilation at the moment when a more perceptive view of their predicament is at last beginning to be possible. Within the past few years there have been indications that the roots of difference within Irish society are being explored with much greater sensitivity and thoroughness than ever before. This exploration has still not displaced political history from pride of place in Irish studies, but enough pioneering work has been done in other fields for these lectures to be based upon the theme that the connection between culture and anarchy is fundamental to the understanding of modern Ireland.

I must quickly make it clear that the connection is not the one that seems implicit in my title, unblushingly borrowed as that is from Matthew Arnold. On the contrary, where Arnold saw culture as a unifying force in a fragmented society and as a barrier against anarchy, my thesis is that in Ireland culture—or rather, the diversity of cultures—has been a force which has worked against the evolution of a homogeneous society and in doing so has been an agent of anarchy rather than of unity. By anarchy I do not mean simply the collapse of law and order, frequent as this has been in one part or other of Ireland over the centuries. I mean rather that the co-existence of several cultures, related yet distinct, has made it difficult, if not impossible, for Irishmen to have a coherent view of themselves in relation to each other and to the outside world. And I would wish to argue that this malaise is both more deep-seated and harder to cure than the political instability with which we are all familiar, and of which it is a prime cause.

In this lecture I want to identify in broad terms the conflicting cultures with which these lectures will be concerned, but first I should make it clear that from my standpoint Arnold's analysis of the role of culture is almost as inadequate as his definition of culture itself. It is not much help to be told that culture is 'a study of perfection', nor to know that the essence of perfection was distilled for him by Swift, who in *The Battle of the Books* singled out as 'the two noblest of things, sweetness and light'. No doubt the ironic Augustan would have been considerably taken aback at the variations woven upon his innocent theme by the eminent Victorian. 'The pursuit of perfection', Arnold pronounced, 'is the pursuit of sweetness and light.' Culture, he says in a famous passage, seeks 'to make the best that has been thought and known in the world current everywhere', and 'to make all men live in an atmosphere of sweetness and light'.[1]

There is a prelapsarian innocence about much of this. When Arnold was composing his essay in the late 1860s, the social sciences were still in their infancy. There were no social anthropologists or social psychologists to compel him to explain himself more intelligibly. The result is that much of what he says conveys to us not merely an impression of 'thinness' (T. S. Eliot's word), but also of irrelevance.[2] Certainly, it is a long time since 'the best that has been thought and known in the world' has been widely current in Ireland, and 'sweetness and light' are not the terms which spring immediately to mind in describing the condition of that unhappy country. To get closer to Irish realities we shall have to interpret culture in a much broader sense, yet without committing ourselves irrevocably to the devotees of any specific school or sect. At this stage, perhaps, it will be enough to apply it to the different groups in Ireland which either have or have had a distinct and relatively autonomous existence and whose members have shared a recognizably common way of life. In identifying such ways of life we shall have to use many different instruments —language and literature, mythology and folklore, history

[1] Matthew Arnold, *Culture and Anarchy, with Friendship's Garland and Some Literary Essays* (ed. R. H. Super, Michigan, 1965), pp. 91, 99, 112, 113.
[2] T. S. Eliot, *Notes Towards the Definition of Culture* (London, 1948), p. 22.

and theology, economics and politics. And we shall seek our evidence of diversity in all the manifold circumstances of Irish life from the furniture of men's kitchens to the furniture of their minds.

This seems a far cry from Matthew Arnold. Yet, when I described him just now as irrelevant I was not being wholly fair. Irrelevant to most modern discussions of culture he may be, but irrelevant to the affairs of Ireland he is not, for he was one of the first Victorians to grasp a central fact about Anglo-Irish relations, that Irishmen were not just second-class Englishmen, but something quite different. Quaintly different, perhaps, or even horridly different, but different.

Much of *Culture and Anarchy*, as we know, is an indictment of certain elements of society, particularly the middle-class Philistines who could not properly exercise power because of their dangerous obsession with 'doing what one likes'.[3] When Arnold was composing his discourses the Fenian disturbances of 1867 in England and Ireland were a sharp reminder of the turmoil just below the surface of Victorian life. Not, Arnold observed ironically, that there was any real danger of anarchy from Fenianism, because

. . . it was never part of our creed that the great right and blessedness of an Irishman, or, indeed, of anybody on earth except an Englishman, is to do as he likes . . . And then, the difference between an Irish Fenian and an English rough is so immense and the case, in dealing with the Fenian, is so much more clear! He is so evidently desperate and dangerous, a man of a conquered race, a papist, with centuries of ill-usage to inflame him against us, with an alien religion established by us at his expense, with no admiration of our institutions, no love of our virtues, no talents for our business, no turn for our comfort! Show him our symbolical Truss Manufactory on the finest site in Europe, and tell him that British industrialism and individualism can bring a man to that, and he remains cold! Evidently, if we deal tenderly with a sentimentalist like this, it is out of pure philanthropy.[4]

This flash of sympathy did not mean that Arnold condoned Fenianism. On the contrary, his political attitude towards Ireland was conservative and he came to regard even Gladstonian Home

[3] Matthew Arnold, *Culture and Anarchy, with Friendship's Garland and Some Literary Essays*, p. 117.
[4] Ibid., pp. 121–2.

Rule as a leap in the dark.[5] But it did suggest that he was capable of regarding the Irish as being other than English. Indeed, he had already indicated as much in the famous lecture 'On the study of Celtic literature', given at Oxford a couple of years earlier. In that lecture Arnold made a gallant attempt, within the limitations of the sources available to him, to characterize what it meant to be Celtic, and to understand what he took to be the romantic or, as he called it, 'Titanic' element in Celtic literature. 'Sentiment' was for him the key to the strange genius of the Celts. 'The Celts', he said, 'with their vehement reaction against the despotism of fact, with their sensuous nature, their manifold striving, their adverse destiny, their immense calamities, the Celts are the prime authors . . . of this Titanism in poetry.'[6] He then, unfortunately, somewhat spoiled the effect of this stirring rhetoric by citing Ossian as a chief example, thus reminding us of what a modern critic has said, that Arnold 'had read many of the best books and apparently all the worst books on Celtic literature and history'.[7]

This did not prevent him from drawing attention to some less desirable attributes. 'The Celt,' he wrote, 'undisciplinable, anarchical, and turbulent of nature, but out of affection and admiration giving himself body and soul to some leader, that is not a promising political temperament, it is just the opposite of the Anglo-Saxon temperament, disciplinable and steadily obedient within certain limits, but retaining an inalienable part of freedom and self-dependence; but it is a temperament for which one has a kind of sympathy notwithstanding.'[8]

Nowadays such generalizations make us wince, for they carry overtones which strike some perhaps hyper-sensitive ears as racialist. If it seems strange that they did not arouse protest at the time, this may have been because the modern descendants of the Celts (if one may use the term of a people so ethnically mongrel

[5] P. J. McCarthy, *Matthew Arnold and the Three Classes* (London and New York, 1964), pp. 155–73.

[6] Matthew Arnold, *Lectures and Essays in Criticism* (ed. R. H. Super, Michigan, 1962), pp. 351, 370.

[7] John V. Kelleher, 'Matthew Arnold and the Celtic Revival', in H. Levin (ed.), *Perspectives of Criticism* (Cambridge, Mass., 1950), pp. 205–6.

[8] Matthew Arnold, *Lectures and Essays in Critiscism*, p. 347.

as the Irish)[9] did not themselves know any better—the 'Celtic twilight' poets of the next generation in Ireland, for example, mostly shared Arnold's ignorance of Celtic languages. But it may also have been due to a certain cynicism. 'The most likely explanation', Professor J. V. Kelleher has suggested, 'is that the Celts and their few friends saw him only as one more of those perennial British reformers . . . who have always been ready to take a shot at solving the Anglo-Celtic question or some aspect of it without hurting anybody. Such Englishmen are always given free rein in the Celtic provinces. It is well known that they don't bite.'[10]

Yet perhaps that is a little harsh. For although Arnold did indeed generalize rashly about Celts in general, towards the Irish in particular he showed both goodwill and responsibility. 'Let us,' he pleaded, 'reunite ourselves with our better mind and with the world through science; and let it be one of our angelic revenges on the Philistines, who among their other sins are the guilty authors of Fenianism, to found at Oxford a chair of Celtic, and to send, through the gentle ministration of science, the message of peace to Ireland.'[11] It is pleasant for an Irishman, just a hundred years after that chair was founded, to acknowledge the generosity with which the University of Oxford, more particularly Jesus College, has responded to Arnold's imaginative proposal.

That one of the foremost critics of the age should thus have held out the hand of friendship to Ireland was itself a striking fact, but one no less striking was that he should have done so on the basis of imperfect science and genuine incomprehension. If this were true of an exceptionally well-informed and sympathetic commentator, it did not augur well for the attitude of Arnold's less educated and less sensitive fellow-countrymen. And that was important because of the extent to which nineteenth-century Ireland existed within the English cultural context. When we

[9] The Celts, in fact, were late arrivals in the centuries before the birth of Christ upon a scene where there had been much migration for several thousand years previously. See especially Frank Mitchell, *The Irish Landscape* (London, 1976), pp. 160–2.

[10] John V. Kelleher, loc. cit., p. 199.

[11] Matthew Arnold, *Lectures and Essays in Criticism*, p. 386.

come to review the different cultures that collided within Irish society, we shall have to bear in mind always that these cultures are principally to be defined not so much by their relations with each other, critical as those were, but by their relations with the English culture under whose shadow they existed and to which they had always to respond. Indeed, it is hardly too much to say that for most of the nineteenth century English culture was the most effective unifying force in Ireland, disguising for many decades—indeed, very nearly destroying—the underlying diversity which was an essential element in the life of the country.[12]

Since by then Ireland had been within the field of influence of English culture for seven hundred years her exposure to that culture had necessarily been intense. But the degree of intensity was greatly heightened after 1800. This was partly due to the linking of the two countries in a political and economic union, partly to the accidental circumstance that the more direct involvement of England in Irish affairs coincided with the rapid rise of an industrial society in the larger island. The growth of modern transport in particular made possible for the first time the widespread distribution in Ireland of mass-produced English goods. Not only that, but the north-east corner of the country was brought into such close communion with the new industry that Belfast became in effect a part of the British economy, having more in common with Liverpool and Glasgow than with its Irish hinterland.

Admittedly, this penetration of the Irish market was not universal. To the end of the nineteenth century the remoter areas of the west and south retained a life-style almost untouched by modernity. We shall see presently how eagerly that life-style was seized upon by some as the last outpost of resistance to the encroaching English culture. But the danger of so regarding such areas was that they came increasingly to seem like reservations where a few tribal survivors lived out a pattern of existence which

[12] To speak of an 'English' as opposed to a 'British' culture may sound strange to some ears, but in Ireland, for most people outside north-east Ulster, the term British has always seemed a little anaemic. They have traditionally seen their relationship with their neighbour as one with England rather than with the broader and more artificial concept, Britain.

time and the machine had long since made anachronistic. The halving of the population by the Famine and the ensuing emigration had affected the western half of the country more seriously than the eastern. And this, together with the steady drift from the country to the towns all over Ireland, had created a people the vast majority of whom were not merely accessible to the material benefits of the neighbouring civilization, but longed for them with an insatiable hunger.

It was not only the material benefits of industrial England that flowed across the Irish Sea. English fashions in dress and speech, English journalism and advertising, English books and plays, English music-hall, English concert programmes and concert artists, English painting, English sports and pastimes—all grew and flourished in an Ireland which, in the second half of the century especially, seemed little more than a province in the empire of Victorian taste.

The principal agency through which this cultural diffusion was achieved was the English language. Irish, in partial decline since the eighteenth century, had been dealt a further grievous blow by the Famine, which had removed large numbers of what remained of the predominantly Irish-speaking population. In 1845, on the eve of that catastrophe, about four million people, or half the population, still spoke Irish as their mother-tongue. Only six years later, in a population reduced to about six and a half million, no more than 23 per cent spoke Irish and only 5 per cent were monolingual in that language.[13] It would be naïve however, to lay this great reversal solely at the door of the Famine, for it had begun earlier and continued afterwards. Even before the Famine the Irish people were well on the way to learning one painful but easily absorbed lesson—that the path to economic advancement, whether in Ireland, Britain, or America, could only be trodden successfully by those who were prepared to exchange the language of the folk-museum for that of the market-place. By the mid-nineteenth century English was already

[13] G. Ó Tuathaigh, *Ireland Before the Famine* (Dublin and London, 1972), pp. 157–8; F. S. L. Lyons, *Ireland Since the Famine* (London, paperback edn., 1973), pp. 88 n.

the language of commerce, of politics, and the law. Irish, by contrast, was coming to be regarded as a badge of poverty and of social inferiority. This lesson had begun to be driven home by the Catholic Church at the end of the eighteenth century when, with the foundation of the college and seminary of Maynooth, English became the normal language of the pulpit and of religious instruction. On the same principle of expediency, Daniel O'Connell, himself the product of an Irish-speaking environment, had turned his back on the language. 'I am sufficiently utilitarian', he proclaimed, 'not to regret its gradual passing.' His own movements for Catholic emancipation and for repeal of the Union further contributed to the decline of Irish, since the mass meetings and the popular propaganda which were central to his agitation were conducted primarily in English.[14]

One other factor in the dissemination of the English language and of English culture in a broad sense was the development of a national system of primary education from the 1830s onward. It is not correct to say, as is still sometimes said in Ireland, that this was the principal device used by an alien government for the deliberate destruction of the Irish language, since, as we have seen, that destruction was being rapidly achieved by other means, but it is true that the national school system, with its aim of making every pupil 'a happy English child' intensified the trend already established.[15]

The creation of this national system of primary education nearly forty years before anything like it was attempted in England is a striking instance of a phenomenon often overlooked in the history of Anglo-Irish relations. This is the fact that Ireland, which in earlier times had derived from England her forms of administration and her legal and political institutions, began in the nineteenth century to be used almost as a social laboratory. That is to say, experiments in governmental regulation were undertaken to a degree that would hardly have been tolerated in the England of that day. The extent of this experimentation can easily be exaggerated, and it would be wrong to

[14] Angus Macintyre, *The Liberator* (London, 1965), pp. 127 and 128 n. 1.
[15] F. S. L. Lyons, *Ireland Since the Famine*, pp. 88–9.

magnify a handful of piece-meal, *ad hoc* arrangements into a grand policy of *étatisme*.[16] Nevertheless, the poverty of Ireland, combined with the fact that there was no large and readily accepted governing class, meant that initiatives from the centre did become necessary from time to time. This was the case, for example, with the creation of a national police force, with the beginnings of a rudimentary health service, and with the various enterprises undertaken by the Board of Works.

It would be easy to deduce from these last that the principal monuments of English rule in Ireland were the jails, courthouses, and lunatic asylums which a grateful successor-state still uses to capacity, but the matter went much deeper. In two fundamental respects the intrusion of the state succeeded in bringing about notable shifts of power within Irish society. The first of these, the disestablishment of the Church of Ireland in 1869, was the logical sequel to the emancipation of Catholics forty years earlier, and it marked decisively, not merely the passing of the privileged position of Anglicanism as the state religion, but the beginning of the end of the Protestant ascendancy in the spiritual and moral leadership of the country.

A year after he had disestablished the Irish church Gladstone passed the Irish Land Act of 1870. Its details are unimportant, for it proved ineffective, but its chief significance remains, that for the first time the imperial parliament had intervened on the side of the tenant against the landlord. The precedent soon broadened out, moving from the concept of partnership in the soil to that of buying out the landlords and converting the tenants into a peasant proprietary. The process was not to be completed until after independence, but already by the beginning of the twentieth century the outcome was plain. The ownership of the land was passing, had to a considerable extent already passed, to those who cultivated it. With this transformation vanished the economic base on which the increasingly precarious authority of the Anglo-Irish gentry had rested for so long.

These major changes could probably only have been accomplished by external pressures, but it would be wrong to think of

[16] O. MacDonagh, *Ireland* (Englewood Cliffs, N.J., 1968), chap. 2.

such pressures as being a product of elaborate planning or even adequate knowledge of the country and its people. Although a series of blue-books laid bare the anatomy of Ireland as never before, there is little evidence that these made much impact, except upon professional administrators and a few committed politicians. Those Englishmen who did go to Ireland brought back descriptions of the place and its inhabitants which often seemed to reflect their authors' predispositions rather than any recognizable Irish reality. These predispositions had been formed, at least in part, by the very nature of the long, uneasy relationship between the two islands. Ireland, after all, was a conquered country, and from their earliest presence there the English, or their Anglo-Norman ancestors, had felt it desirable to justify that presence by emphasizing the primitive savagery of the society they had displaced. Thus the war of conquest, when it was seriously undertaken in the sixteenth and seventeenth centuries, was easily defined as a conflict between 'civilization' and 'barbarism'. The fact that this coincided with the Reformation had the further unhappy consequence that 'Protestantism' became identified with 'civilization' and 'Catholicism' with 'barbarism'.[17]

Naturally, the Irish resented this stereotype. Against the accusation of barbarism they constructed a consoling image (which had, indeed, a foundation in fact) of an ancient civilization, a land of saints and scholars, a commitment to monastic Christianity that had laid much of Europe in its debt. And against the almost casual English assumption of superiority they opposed a highly artificial concept of nationality which stressed alike their difference from their English masters and their aspiration towards complete independence of them. But since the expression of that nationality took a violent form from time to time, this only reinforced the English view that the Irish were a brutal people, a view already well entrenched by the long history of agrarian warfare whereby, since the eighteenth century, the dispossessed peasants had waged a subterranean campaign against their landlords or their more fortunate fellows.

It is hardly surprising that the accounts of Ireland which filtered

[17] Patrick O'Farrell, *Ireland's English Question* (London, 1975), chap. 1.

through to England for much of the nineteenth century were far
from flattering. Influenced in some cases by the fashionable ethno-
centric ideas of the age, but more often by the simple spectacle of
Irish misery, they struck a consistently depressing note. The Irish,
it seemed, were friendly but unreliable, volatile but subservient to
their clergy, and combined a peasant shrewdness with an almost
Asiatic poverty. To Carlyle, the Westport workhouse at the close
of the Famine was 'the acme' of 'human swinery'.[18] To Charles
Kingsley, the miserable wretches he saw by the roadside in 1860
seemed, if anything, lower in the scale. ' . . . I am haunted by the
human chimpanzees I saw along that hundred miles of horrible
country. I don't believe they are our fault. I believe there are not
only more of them than of old, but that they are happier, better,
more comfortably fed and lodged under our rule than they ever
were. But to see white chimpanzees is dreadful; if they were black,
one would not feel it so much, but their skins, except where tan-
ned by exposure, are as white as ours.'[19] To Froude, they were
'more like tribes of squalid apes than human beings'.[20] To General
Gordon in 1880, their state seemed worse than that of any other
people in the world, 'living on the verge of starvation in places in
which we would not keep our cattle'.[21]

Mingled with the revulsion which these animal standards
inspired was a sense of guilt, real, even though confused and intermittent. There were always Englishmen, including some of those
most convinced of the inferiority of the Irish, who felt responsible
for this degradation and were anxious to mitigate it. *How* to
mitigate it, few of them had the remotest idea. Ireland seemed
doomed by a malignant fate to occupy the very worst position in
the English scale of operations—too distant to be understood, too
close to be ignored. Proximity and history alike seemed to
dictate a policy of assimilation which might eventually raise the
country to the status of an English region, admittedly poor and
backward compared with most others, but broadly within the

[18] Thomas Carlyle, *Reminiscences of My Irish Journey* (London, 1882), p. 201.

[19] *Charles Kingsley, His Letters and Memories of His Life*, ed. by his wife (London,
1877), ii. 107.

[20] Cited in L. P. Curtis, *Anglo-Saxons and Celts* (Bridgeport, Conn.), p. 85.

[21] *The Times*, 3 Dec. 1880.

same context and with the same cultural values. But distance and stubborn reality had a short way with such dreams. Ireland remained obstinately unlike England—with a land system which took a century of investigation and reform to unravel; a social structure that left a yawning chasm where the industrial middle class ought to have been;[22] a dumb attachment to a Church which in most Englishmen inspired an almost instinctive revulsion; and a prefabricated notion of history where what had actually happened seemed lost in the swirling mists of nostalgia and mythology. Yet, since what had actually happened had included the conquest of the smaller by the larger, the temptation for the larger to lose patience with the vagaries of the smaller was always present. This tendency, reinforced by genuine doubt about how to deal with a problem which seemed familiar but was in fact outside the normal range of English experience, helps to explain the fluctuations of policy from indifference to reform to coercion, and back again to indifference.

Indifference, it is true, became less easy to maintain from the Union onwards. Since Ireland was compensated for the loss of her own parliament by representation at Westminster, she was impelled into her neighbour's politics and from the days of O'Connell the votes and requirements of the Irish members became (if the Hibernicism may be excused) a constant variable

[22] There was indeed a middle class which was growing rapidly in the later nineteenth century, but, leaving aside the special case of north-east Ulster (for which, see lecture 5 below), it bore little resemblance to the English middle class. Over most of the country it consisted mainly of shopkeepers, publicans, and clerks, with some of the larger farmers and a sprinkling of professional people. In Dublin the professional element was more numerous and important (including as it did, many civil servants besides the leading doctors and lawyers), as were also the owners and managers of the service industries, the financial institutions, and the various retail trades. Broadly speaking, the 'shopocracy' and the publicans were Catholics, though the largest and most fashionable stores in Dublin were generally in Protestant hands. Protestants and Catholics mingled in the professions and the civil service, though even there Protestants were probably dominant until at least the 1880s. Being so largely urban and therefore easily accessible, the middle class, whether Protestant or Catholic, was particularly susceptible to English culture, especially in its more popular and vulgar forms. But like the middle class everywhere, it also produced most of the rebels who, as we shall see later, mocked at its *mores* and repudiated its values.

with which English parties had to reckon. In two other ways, also, an Irish influence reached out to affect the English view of the troublesome island. During the nineteenth century Ireland became a mother country, and the dispersion of her people, especially the great exodus to America, made the Irish question an international question to such a degree that as time went on English solutions had increasingly to take account of foreign reactions.

More important even than this in shaping English attitudes and policy was the influx of the Irish into Britain. Congregated in the most squalid slums, working at the worst jobs for the lowest wages, practising their suspect religion, lacking in familial restraint and even in the ordinary decencies of behaviour, dirty and a constant threat to the health and well-being of others, apt to be alarmingly pugnacious when drunk, they—or rather that lowest stratum of them on which hostile critics fastened greedily—were everything Englishmen did not want as neighbours.[23] And since they also imported into England their own brand of violence, it was difficult not to feel that this constituted a threat to the general stability of society, as indeed it occasionally did. A direct consequence of this increasing fear of the Irishman as the harbinger of coming disaster was that the popular view of him began to change. From the likeable buffoon, the stage Irishman, the Handy Andy, the good-natured but thick-headed Paddy with a charmingly bizarre turn of phrase, he became, from about the 1860s onward, a kind of monster depicted in the cartoons of the day with simian or porcine features, and festooned with weapons, a vivid reminder that decent English citizens stood in mortal peril. The land war kept this bloodthirsty image alive and the Phoenix Park murders in May 1882 probably marked its climax. Two weeks after that event, Tenniel published in *Punch* perhaps the

[23] Two points need to be made by way of balance. One is that the Irish did not create the appalling conditions they experienced in the early industrial cities, though they undoubtedly contributed to them. The other is that there is a substantial body of evidence to show that towards the end of the nineteenth century they had achieved a high degree of assimilation, even though their clannish solidarity still often made them disliked. Both these points are well documented in J. A. Jackson, *The Irish in Britain* (London, 1963), especially chaps. 3, 4, and 7.

most famous of his anti-Irish cartoons. Called 'The Irish Franken-stein', it showed a demoralized Parnell crouching in the back-ground, while in the foreground loomed a huge Caliban-like figure, armed to the teeth and with a bloodstained knife in one hand to drive home the lesson of how Lord Frederick Cavendish and Under-Secretary Burke had perished. By the end of the century, when quieter times had come, such dehumanizing portraits gradually fell out of fashion, but for some of the most critical years of the Union between the two countries, from about 1860 to about 1890, an indelible image of Irish savagery had been stamped on the minds of the English reading public.[24]

This is not to say that those who knew the Irish question more intimately did not take a more discriminating view. They were aware that Ireland did not fit easily into the British pattern of life and they were able to identify some of her more obvious peculiari-ties—for example, the rivalry of Catholic and Protestant; the tension between landlords of mainly English descent and tenants who, after centuries, still hungered for their land; the absence of industrialism and of an industrial middle class, except in the north-east of the country; the strange contrast between the constant clamour that Ireland was a nation and the persistent tendency of individual Irishmen to swarm out of that nation in their hundreds of thousands in pursuit of a living, any living, anywhere.

Beyond these commonplaces few observers had time or in-clination to penetrate. Perhaps the most serious indictment of the English rulers of Ireland during the whole period of the Union was their failure to appreciate the complexity of a problem which they constantly distorted by over-simplification. The fact that English culture was so dominant in nineteenth-century Ireland no doubt partly explains and justifies this tendency to see the situation in clear-cut black and white. If a majority of the Irish insisted on behaving as if they were Englishmen (inferior Englishmen, of course) then it seemed only civil to take them at their word. But

[24] Professor L. P. Curtis, Jr. has thrown much light on English attitudes to the Irish in two books—*Anglo-Saxons and Celts* cited above and *Apes and Angels* (Washington, 1971).

if they were to be regarded as Englishmen then their demand
for independence, their obsession with the question of national
identity, fell into a new and diminishing perspective. In the face of
such apparent inconsistency Englishmen not unnaturally found it
difficult to treat Irish assertions of separateness and difference as
seriously as they deserved. Thus, the relationship between the two
countries, always of paramount importance to the Irish, was only
intermittently so to the English, preoccupied as the latter were by
a multitude of vaster imperial concerns.

Another way of putting this is to say that the Irish problem
dropped out of English consciousness except when the Irish
themselves succeeded in reinserting it. Unhappily, as they quickly
discovered, the most effective way of doing so was by the threat
or actuality of physical force. This in turn confirmed the English
in their belief that the Irish had an inveterate addiction to violence,
which could only be cured, or at least held in check, by vigorous
counter-measures of repression. Not until the closing decades of
the nineteenth century were ameliorating policies vigorously
applied, and then largely in the hope of distracting Irish opinion
from the will-o'-the-wisp of Home Rule. The alternative of
'resolute government' never came near to being applied for the
twenty years which Lord Salisbury had judged necessary, for the
simple reason that the ups and downs of English party politics
would not permit it. Nor, in fairness, should it be forgotten that
there were many Englishmen who preferred to put their faith in
constructive reform and who in fact succeeded in bringing about
more of such reform than an Irish parliament might have achieved
had Home Rule been granted when it was first demanded in the
1870s and 1880s.

Yet neither coercion nor conciliation worked. Their failure was
due only in part to the lack of continuity in British policy. Much
more, I believe, was it due to an inadequate knowledge and understanding of the profound cultural differences which not only
divided Ireland from England, but also divided Irishmen from
each other. In concluding this lecture I want to anticipate what I
hope to deal with subsequently in more detail, by suggesting that
the true complexity of the Irish question in its modern form has

derived from the fact that at least four cultures have for the last three centuries been jostling each other in the island.[25]

The dominant culture, as I have already indicated, was the English culture, imposing itself initially by conquest, establishing itself by successive colonizations, entrenching itself in law and government, developing new economic and social relationships, exercising a constant influence upon habits of thought and modes of life. Since this culture was so dominant, it was easy for Englishmen to assume that others, so far as they could be discerned at all, were merely local or regional variants upon the grand English theme. But although there was a sense in which this was so—each of the other cultures had no option but to relate closely to the dominant one—they nevertheless remained obstinately, if at times obscurely, different.

This was perhaps most true of the native culture, whose representatives at the end of the nineteenth century accounted for about three-quarters of the population. An English observer confronted with this culture could without much difficulty have distinguished certain of its characteristics which would have struck him as in some way 'foreign'. That it had an ancient Gaelic base was still clear, though it appeared that the Irish language, literature and customs were nearly everywhere in retreat. That it was deeply, indeed ostentatiously, Catholic was obvious, but that Catholicism too seemed foreign, for its intense, puritanical cast of mind was worlds away from the discreet and altogether more genteel article that passed for Catholicism in England. That it was predominantly rural in character was easy to see, but our English observer would have found the Irish countryside a great deal bleaker and more intimidating than the home counties. A backward agriculture, a

[25] I say 'at least four cultures', because a different principle of selection could easily add others. It would be quite legitimate, for example, to explore the contrast between the cities, especially Dublin, and the rest of the country, or between the market-towns and their rural hinterlands, or, on a larger scale, to investigate the division between east and west as well as that between north and south. In these lectures, however, which are concerned primarily with conflict between the main cultural traditions in the island, I have sought deliberately to emphasize what divided one tradition from another and have therefore left largely (though not entirely) on one side the variations, regional and otherwise, that undoubtedly existed within each of these traditions.

peasantry which, though hospitable in its instincts, was impoverished and embittered by the long struggle against a hostile environment and an inequitable land system, above everything a society where ancient beliefs and superstitions still had an almost elemental power—all of this was vastly different from the compact, well-ordered, intensely cultivated farmlands familiar over much of England. Finally, this native Irish culture, so far as it had produced a political philosophy, seemed to have opted for something called 'nationalism', which to an outsider was a confusing label that apparently applied simultaneously and equally to treason-felony, and to parliamentary agitation, yet, strangely, did not inhibit large numbers of Irishmen, some of whom called themselves nationalists, from serving the Crown in many capacities inside and outside their own country. In face of such confusions and contradictions, it was easy to assume that the native culture had lost its impetus, and that in the ordinary course of events it would be wholly absorbed by the all-embracing English culture. A large part of the history of modern Ireland between the fall of Parnell and the death of Yeats was to be concerned with the testing of this assumption in the light of a Gaelic revival as unexpected as it was brilliant and precarious.

If native Ireland was likely to strike an observer from outside as noticeably 'foreign', he could have been expected to feel more at home among the descendants of the English settlers in Ireland, to whom, about the end of the nineteenth century, the name 'Anglo-Irish' was beginning to be attached. That name was not of their seeking, though it expresses very precisely the schizophrenia which was their natural condition. They had habitually called themselves simply 'Irish' and in their eighteenth-century heyday had even monopolized the term, to the exclusion of the native and Catholic Irish whose legal existence the penal laws had then scarcely acknowledged. On the other hand, conscious that they were a privileged minority, separated by race and religion from those whose land their ancestors had seized, they still looked to England as their ultimate protector and regarded themselves as members of an empire which they were proud to serve. This divided loyalty led them eventually into the characteristic dilemma of a colonial governing class, torn between their country of origin and their country of settlement. In the last decades of the eighteenth century they had asserted a spurious independence, claiming for the Irish parliament, which they dominated completely, a degree of autonomy from British rule. Yet when their position was menaced by the insurrection of 1798, they not only joined with the British forces in suppressing it, but acquiesced in the destruction of the Irish parliament in return for what they hoped would be the greater security of the Union. This may well have been their fatal mistake, for it increased both their dependence upon a British connection which proved not to be dependable, and their alienation from their fellow-countrymen who regarded them as more than ever the English garrison in Ireland.

So far as there was a governing class in Ireland it was the gentry who provided it. Never very numerous and seldom very wealthy, they nevertheless had important English connections.[26] Some of the grandest families had estates in both countries, intermarried with the English aristocracy, and frequently rose high in the imperial service. Even the less glittering county families who formed the bulk of the gentry found the normal outlet for their younger sons in the forces of the Crown. Below them in the social scale, but possibly of more importance in the economic life of the country, and certainly a more vital force in its intellectual life, was a professional and entrepreneurial class which had an influence out of all proportion to its exiguous numbers. But, as always in Ireland, it is dangerous to postulate a rigid class system.

[26] Although the gentry were spread all over Ireland, their position in the south was much more vulnerable because Protestants as a whole were less numerous than in the north. In Ulster, by 1911, Protestants, of all varieties and classes, numbered nearly 60 per cent of the total population. In the other three provinces they accounted for only about 10 per cent. These southern Protestants were almost, though not quite wholly, synonymous with southern unionism. Although some of them belonged to the middle class, and a few to the working class in the towns, there seems no reason to dispute the verdict of the leading authority on the subject that 'southern unionists tended to be not only Protestant and anglicized, but also aristocratic and landed, with a leavening of Roman Catholic landowners, intellectuals from Trinity College and prominent businessmen' (Patrick Buckland, *Irish Unionism: The Anglo-Irish and the New Ireland, 1885–1922* (Dublin and London, 1972), pp. xiv, xx).

The sons of the gentry and the sons of the clergy and the barristers mingled freely at school and at the university, though solicitors and doctors still occupied a more ambiguous position and 'trade' was of course beyond the pale. School in the eighteenth century had generally meant one of the sound if unspectacular Irish foundations, but in the nineteenth century it meant increasingly a public school in England, a fact which had an important bearing, still too little realized, upon the growing alienation of the Anglo-Irish from the land of their birth. As for the university, it could only mean Oxford, Cambridge, or Trinity College, Dublin.

Trinity College occupied a special place in the affections of the Anglo-Irish and was indeed the chief bastion of their culture. Founded in the sixteenth century as a means of civilizing the 'wild Irish', it had always been the preserve of the ruling élite. For although Catholics had been admitted to degrees in 1793 and to Fellowships and Scholarships eighty years later, Trinity had quite consciously remained an ascendancy institution, concerned not only with educating young men for lay careers—often in the British or Indian Civil Services—but also with the training of the clergy of the Church of Ireland. And since even after its disestablishment that Church retained a considerable amount of its wealth and social prestige, the link between Anglicanism and the university emphasized the exclusiveness of the latter, though from about 1875 onwards this was intensified by the action of the Irish Catholic bishops in forbidding members of their Church to attend such an infidel College without a special dispensation.

What then was the essence of this Anglo-Irish culture, and how far did it differ from the dominant English culture? It is not easy to answer these questions precisely because they are questions which seldom seem to have occurred to the Anglo-Irish themselves. When, in subsequent lectures, we watch some of them attempting to define their culture, or to fuse it with the Gaelic culture, we shall have to remember always that these innovators were a small minority drawn mainly from the middle class rather than from the gentry. For most of the latter their Anglo-Irishness was unconscious, though that did not make it any less real. What distinguished them from their English counterparts was long residence and much intermarriage with the native population in a country which differed from England in its climate, in the quality of its soil and its system of land tenure, in its social organization—above all, perhaps, in the insecurity of life and the uncertainty of the future.

All these influences affected the Anglo-Irish in diverse ways. At one level they gave a passable imitation of a governing class on the English model. They acted as deputy lieutenants of their counties, as high sheriffs or as justices of the peace, and they were prominent in local government until the end of the nineteenth century. Apart from visits to the Dublin Horse Show and to the winter season at the Viceregal Court, many of them resided all the year round in their Georgian houses—sometimes beautiful, sometimes ugly, but often dilapidated and generally uncomfortable—where they lived the sort of life that landlords lived everywhere. Shooting, fishing, and hunting, interspersed with hospitality frequently more lavish than they could afford—this was the framework of their lives. Worship of the horse was universal and the late Brendan Behan, when he christened them 'the Horse Protestants', hit the nail exactly on the head. Books, unless they had to do with angling or the turf, were not widely read in their households, though some had splendid libraries dating mainly from the eighteenth century. Religion—usually of an evangelical Protestant strain, though there were also some Catholics among the gentry—was strictly practised, varying, however, between the genteel and the brimstone.

This seems on the surface not so very different from the placid existence of an English squire. Yet at another level the Anglo-Irish gentry had to endure a situation which an English squire could scarcely begin to comprehend. With the rise of nationalism in the nineteenth century, they found themselves shut out from what might otherwise have seemed their natural role in Irish politics, and this at a time when the ground on which they had stood for generations, their ownership of the land, was beginning to quake under them. Their dependence on the British connection naturally increased, and this in turn reinforced their tendency to seek employment in the service of an empire to which they could give

a loyalty that the newly emerging Ireland did not seem to want.
A modern historian, Professor Beckett, has suggested that two of
their most striking characteristics were arrogance and ambivalence.[27] To the extent that this was true, both qualities were
probably the product of their isolation. If they were arrogant it
was because it had been their fate to govern a people which, for
much of its history, had shown little capacity to govern itself. If
they were ambivalent, it was because, although they were 'of
Ireland', and thought of themselves as Irish, they were doomed
never to penetrate the Catholic and Gaelic recesses of Irishness, and
could not afford to sever their ties with Englishness, in which a
part of their nature found its deepest fulfilment. The tension that
this duality introduced into their lives was faithfully reflected in
their literature which often alternated, even in the same writer (for
example, Swift at one end of the tradition and Yeats at the other),
between the overcharged rhetoric of assertion, and the sardonic
irony of withdrawal.

Their tragedy was that, hesitating as they did between two
worlds, they could never be fully accepted by either. To the
English they came increasingly to seem an anachronism, to the
Irish they remained an excrescence. Caught between unsym-
pathetic governments and resentful tenants they provided a convenient scapegoat for most of the ills of nineteenth-century
Ireland. The popular stereotype of the Anglo-Irish landlord as a
callous, rack-renting, evicting absentee, living in luxury on the
pittances squeezed from hungry peasants, became so widely
believed that it is only recently that it has begun to be questioned.
Certainly, there was absenteeism, there were some rack-renters
and eviction—more commonly, the threat of eviction—was
always in the background. But landlords proceeded to extremes
much less than used to be supposed and the agrarian malaise lay
much deeper, in the lack of capital for investment in the land, lack
of opportunity to put it to work, and lack of return in the shape
of improved and more productive farming.[28]

---

[27] J. C. Beckett, *The Anglo-Irish Tradition* (London, 1976), pp. 143–7.

[28] For evidence of this reassessment, see James S. Donnelly, *The Land and the
People of Nineteenth Century Cork: the Rural Economy and the Land Question*

The consequence was that although superficially relations between landlords and their tenants were often amicable, and although farm and domestic servants were easy to come by—the Irish nanny was as much a pillar of pre-revolutionary Ireland as the negro mammy was of the ante-bellum American South—the gentry remained isolated from the life around them. It is no accident that the Big House and the Protestant Church, though dominating their little society and closely involved with it, were still not part of an integrated community, or that in the whole of Ireland the number of villages which would have fitted into the English landscape without comment could almost have been counted on the fingers of one hand. The Anglo-Irish ruling class were, from the Famine onwards, living on borrowed time. With the economic depression of the 1870s, the ensuing land agitation, and the steady conversion of successive British governments towards a policy of expropriation, their days were numbered.[29]

Against this sombre diagnosis it may be objected that the Protestant minority to which they belonged was a substantial one, amounting to not less than a quarter of the whole population of Ireland. Was not this a guarantee of stability and permanence? Viewed from outside, it may well have seemed so, but once again the external view is misleading. The great majority of Irish Protestants were concentrated in the province of Ulster. Taking that province, in its historic sense, to consist of nine counties, we find that in 1861 (when the post-Famine demographic pattern had clearly emerged) out of a total for the whole of Ireland of 693,000 'Episcopalian Protestants', some 56 per cent

---

(London, 1975), pp. 173–218; Barbara L. Solow, *The Land Question and the Irish Economy, 1870–1903* (Cambridge, Mass., 1971), pp. 51–88; W. E. Vaughan, 'Landlord and Tenant Relations in Ireland Between the Famine and the Land War, 1850–78', in L. M. Cullen and T. C. Smart (ed.), *Comparative Aspects of Scottish and Irish Economic and Social History, 1600–1900* (Edinburgh, 1976), pp. 216–26, and W. E. Vaughan, 'An Assessment of the Economic Performance of Irish Landlords, 1851–81', in R. Hawkins and F. S. L. Lyons (ed.), *Ireland Under the Union: Varieties of Tension* (Oxford, 1979), chap. 6.

[29] For a sensitive and authoritative view of the Anglo-Irish, see T. R. Henn, *The Lonely Tower* (London, paperback edn., 1966), chap. 1; also the same author's semi-autobiographical lecture, 'The Big House', in T. R. Henn, *Last Essays* (Gerrard's Cross, 1976), pp. 207–20.

lived in Ulster; fifty years later, of a total Episcopalian population of 577,000, about 62 per cent lived in Ulster. And even these were not quite so numerous as the Presbyterians, who numbered just over half a million in 1861 and about 440,000 in 1911, almost all of whom belonged to the northern province. By that latter date, it would be broadly correct to say that in the nine Ulster counties Presbyterians and Episcopalians together (788,000) outnumbered the Roman Catholics (691,000), but that of the two main Protestant denominations the Presbyterians were somewhat larger than the Episcopalians.[30]

Behind these figures lies a fact of crucial importance to the clash of cultures in Ireland. It can best be expressed by the paradox that, while in one sense this juxtaposition of denominations made Ulster seem a microcosm of the cultural diversity of the country as a whole, in another sense it supported the argument that Ulster had always been a special case. In a later lecture we shall see that there are grounds for viewing it as having been a special case from its earliest beginnings, but here it is enough to indicate that at least since the seventeenth century certain circumstances had intensified its particularity. These may be summed up in three words—conquest, Calvinism, and industrialization. Because it was the last of the Irish provinces to be colonized, because the colonization had resulted not in the displacement of the native population, but in the loss of their land and status, and because the newcomers were English Episcopalians and Scottish Presbyterians, different races and religions were confined within 'the narrow ground' of the province.[31] But because conquest resulted in Protestant ascendancy, and because the Presbyterians emerged as the largest Protestant community, the ethos of the ascendancy was predominantly Presbyterian. With the coming of industrialism in the nineteenth century this ethos became if anything more pronounced, since it was the Presbyterians who were mostly strongly represented among the entrepreneurs who built the docks and

---

[30] Summarized from F. S. L. Lyons, *Ireland Since the Famine*, pp. 18, 23.

[31] The expression 'the narrow ground' was first applied to Ulster by Sir Walter Scott and has lately been used by A. T. Q. Stewart as the title of a perceptive study of the Ulster question (*The Narrow Ground*, London, 1977).

shipyards and linen mills on which Belfast rose to its precarious prosperity.

From this history there evolved a deeply divided society, but one whose members had perhaps more in common than they were generally prepared to admit. Most other Irishmen recognized in the Ulsterman certain characteristics which seemed quintessentially northern and independent of any denominational allegiance. These included a capacity for hard work, an incapacity for compromise, a hard common sense, a due regard for the importance both of religion and of money, a mordant turn of humour combined with a native kindliness and a respect for the domestic virtues. Yet, if these were qualities which Ulstermen held in common, there was no escaping the fact that this was a strongly Protestant province, albeit one in which different kinds of Protestants eyed each other suspiciously across a wide cultural divide. The Anglican Church of Ireland was, in Ulster as elsewhere, the Church of the landowners and the traditional governing class, though it was also the Church of many independent farmers and even, as a result of nineteenth-century evangelical zeal, of substantial numbers of the Belfast working population. The Presbyterians drew their strength both from the market-towns and farming communities in the east of the province, and from the middle class of professional and business people in Belfast, and to a lesser extent in Londonderry. It was these people who supplied much of the dynamism of nineteenth-century Ulster and it was they who set their stamp upon the quality of life. The gospels of work and thrift and cleanliness and godliness were preached and practised with an impressive severity. They were a serious people, caring for education, devoting themselves to their businesses, turning their faces against the flesh and the devil, seeing anti-Christ in the Pope of Rome, cherishing tribal fears of Catholic insurgence that went back to the seventeenth century, and each July abandoning themselves to tribal rejoicing at the deliverance wrought by King William at the Boyne in 1690.

Between these Protestants and those of the south there was little contact and less affection. Denied their full civil rights in the eighteenth century, the Presbyterians nursed a long-standing resentment against the ascendancy class, from which they were profoundly different, in church doctrine and organization, as also in social structure and intellectual outlook. True, Trinity College afforded a meeting-place for the two traditions, and both Anglicans and Presbyterians shared the same anxieties about the rising tide of nineteenth-century Catholicism and nationalism. But their cultures, as we shall see later, were strikingly incompatible and, at a critical moment in their history, the divergences between them would be more potent than the need to combine against a common enemy.

I end then by stressing once again that the key to the Irish problem in its modern form was the competitive co-existence within Ireland, not just of a simple dualism between native and settler, but of a complex of Irish and Anglo-Irish cultures operating within, and powerfully affected by, the dominant English culture. This was not novel—on the contrary, it had been implicit, and sometimes explicit, in the evolution of Ireland since the seventeenth century. But it was to be brought into much sharper focus by a combination of chance and choice which a new situation began to offer in or about 1890. That new situation, and the various responses it evoked, will be explored in my next two lectures.

2

After Parnell

'The modern literature of Ireland, and indeed all that
stir of thought which prepared for the Anglo-Irish
war, began when Parnell fell from power in 1891. A
disillusioned and embittered Ireland turned from
parliamentary politics; an event was conceived; and
the race began, as I think, to be troubled by that
event's long gestation.' (W. B. Yeats, *Autobiographies*,
p. 559.)

MAX BEERBOHM once remarked of Dr Johnson that while he had a
way of being right, he also had a way of being wrong. Yeats, in
the quotation at the head of this lecture, went one better by con-
triving to be both right and wrong at the same time. He was
right in seizing on the death of Parnell in 1891 as a symbolic event,
right in sensing that Irish energy, so long concentrated upon the
drive for Home Rule, found new goals and new modes of
expression in the generation between the fall of 'the Chief' and the
Easter Rising of 1916. This extraordinary transference of energy
from the life of politics into the life of culture was to make the city
of Dublin a place of world importance for a brief time. In this
lecture and the next I shall be examining both the transformation
of energy and the explosions which resulted therefrom, for both
are central to my thesis that in modern Ireland culture has been
a divisive rather than a reconciling influence.

First, however, it has to be said that in one important sense
Yeats was wrong in his chronology. The stir of thought which he
observed in the years after 1891, and to which he himself contributed so much, would not have been possible had not a trail
been marked out by others in a more remote past. It was a trail

which began with amateur investigations into the literature and
antiquities of Ireland in the seventeenth and eighteenth centuries,
but which developed into something of much greater moment
when the Royal Irish Academy was founded in 1785. That
institution has remained at the centre of the serious study of Irish
civilization ever since, for although all sorts of more or less
ephemeral societies sprang up with similar objectives, none of them
competed with the Academy, which laid down the standards of
scholarship that by the end of the nineteenth century had made
'Celtic' or Irish studies a rigorous discipline attracting continental
as well as local scholars of the highest calibre.[1]

From the beginning the odour of antiquarianism hung heavy
over these studies. They were a necessary foundation for further
progress, but they did little or nothing to restore Irish as a living
language. On the contrary, even as the scholars laboured, the forces
of change which we have already noted—the Famine, emigration,
the overwhelming pull of English as the sole means of access to
economic betterment and to the dominant culture—were working
in the opposite direction. So obvious had this become that the
mass of the population had recoiled from Irish as a badge of
inferiority to be discarded as quickly as possible. Hence the
seeming paradox that the earliest stages of the revival were
largely the preserve of members of the Anglo-Irish ascendancy.

This was not just the condescension of a governing class amusing
itself with quaint native antiquities. Their concern with the ancient
civilization of Ireland was perfectly genuine, though it was not
wholly disinterested. Few of them seriously contemplated the
restoration of the Irish language as part of the common currency
of educated people, but they did see in the revival of Irish studies
in general a means of attaching themselves to their native country
and at the same time of holding at arm's length the English connection which the more perceptive of them already sensed to be
both dangerous and unreliable.

The case of Sir Samuel Ferguson is crucial here. Ferguson was
born in Belfast in 1810 of a decayed landed family. After three

[1] For the role of the Academy and for the work of individual pioneers, see
W. I. Thompson, *The Imagination of an Insurrection* (New York, 1967), chap. 1.

years at Trinity College, Dublin, he emerged without a degree and
with a vague notion of combining journalism and the law. His
opinions were impeccably Anglican and Tory, and like many of
his generation he was much alarmed by the upsurge of Catholic
nationalism under O'Connell. Their fears found an outlet from
1833 onwards in a new periodical, the *Dublin University Magazine*,
whose first editor was Isaac Butt. Nearly forty years later Butt was
to gain fame as the progenitor of Home Rule, but in the 1830s he
and the authors he gathered round him were chiefly concerned
with safeguarding the Protestant ascendancy in the aftermath of
Catholic emancipation. The Belfast Orangeman in Ferguson
responded to this situation in a way that at once looked back to the
eighteenth century and forward to the twentieth. In one of his
earliest pieces for the *Magazine*, 'A Dialogue between the Head
and Heart of an Irish Protestant', he revealed the classical paranoia
of the Anglo-Irish settler:

Deserted by the Tories, insulted by the Whigs, threatened by the Radicals,
hated by the Papists, and envied by the Dissenters, plundered in our country-
seats, robbed in our town houses, driven abroad by violence, called back by
humanity, and, after all, told that we are neither English nor Irish, fish nor
flesh, but a peddling colony, a forlorn advanced guard that must conform to
every mutinous movement of the pretorian (*sic*) rabble—all this, too, while we
are the acknowledged possessors of nine-tenths of the property of a great
country, and wielders of the preponderating influence between two parties;
on whose relative position depend the greatest interests in the empire.[2]

The ideal solution, he believed, would be to mount a brisk
campaign of proselytism to wean the natives from their foolish
superstitions. But since this was impracticable, and because his love
of the country and its people was perfectly genuine, he conceived
instead a different approach. The only way, he thought, in which
the Anglo-Irish could consolidate their position, given that they
could not count upon British support, was to identify themselves with the Irish past much more thoroughly than hitherto.
Essentially, they should do this by taking the lead in recovering

[2] Samuel Ferguson, 'A Dialogue Between the Head and Heart of an Irish
Protestant', in *Dublin University Magazine* (Nov. 1833), p. 591. See also Malcolm
Brown, *Sir Samuel Ferguson* (Bucknell University Press, New Jersey, 1973),
pp. 39–42.

that past. Through the Royal Irish Academy Ferguson met another young Protestant antiquarian, George Petrie, one of the great collectors of Irish manuscripts, and through Petrie he met the two leading Irish scholars of the day, Eugene O'Curry and John O'Donovan. Under their influence he began to learn Irish himself and was soon heavily committed. This came about almost by chance. In 1831 an Irish scholar, James Hardiman, a Catholic and nationalist of the school of O'Connell, published an anthology of Gaelic lyrics (originals and translations side by side) called *Irish Minstrelsy*, in the course of which he attacked the Anglo-Irish as alien exploiters of a country not their own.

Ferguson reacted to these aspersions in two quite different ways. At one level, he almost conceded Hardiman's point, while suggesting a remedy. 'The Protestants of Ireland', he admitted, 'are wealthy and intelligent beyond most classes of their numbers, in the world; but their wealth has hitherto been insecure, because their intelligence has not embraced a thorough knowledge of the genius and disposition of their Catholic fellow-citizens. The genius of a people at large is not to be learned by the notes of Sunday tourists. The history of centuries must be gathered, published, studied and digested.'[3]

This work was in fact begun a few years later by the Ordnance Survey of Ireland, which brought together a group of scholars and writers to salvage as much as could be recovered of the old Gaelic culture. The group included George Petrie, the two experts, O'Curry and O'Donovan, and also the eccentric and melancholy poet, James Clarence Mangan, whom both Yeats and Joyce acknowledged as a formative influence on their work. But Ferguson's other response to Hardiman's strictures was much more individual and unexpected. To demonstrate what an Anglo-Irishman could do he published his own translations of some of the pieces in *Irish Ministrelsy*. These were not only much better than Hardiman's, they led Ferguson on to other translations which,

---

[3] These remarks occur in the first section of a four-part review which appeared in the *Dublin University Magazine*, in the issues for April, August, October, and November 1834. See also Lady Ferguson, *Sir Samuel Ferguson in the Ireland of His Day* (London, 2 vols., 1896), i. 39–40.

either in his hands or in those of his successors, revealed a wealth of poetic material so long forgotten as to be almost unknown. This material was far older than the seventeenth- and eighteenth-century lyrics which were Hardiman's stock-in-trade. It was the bardic poetry, embodying the legends and sagas of Ireland's pre-Christian, heroic age. Again and again, Ferguson returned to these epic tales, especially to the Ulster or Red Branch cycle whose central figure was Cuchulainn. The results, as poetry, grew less impressive as he grew older and much of his work is now unread, even by specialists. The reason may be that in the latter part of his life Ferguson opted for social respectability rather than for intellectual adventure. Marrying into the Guinness family, he moved increasingly within the frozen inner circle of the Protestant ascendancy, composed of Anglican divines, Trinity dons, eminent physicians, and Q.C.s. He developed a passion for archaeology, became President of the Royal Irish Academy, was knighted and died in the odour of sanctity in 1886. No wonder that, as Yeats observed, a certain 'hardness and heaviness crept into his rhythm'. Nevertheless, it was Yeats who called him 'the most Irish' of poets and Yeats who, in a famous phrase, wished posterity to number him with Ferguson and Mangan, and also with Thomas Davis, of whom more in a moment. We need not take this praise too seriously, for nothing could ever have turned Ferguson into a great poet. Yet his niche in history is secure. Not only did his discovery of the ancient sagas help to prepare the way for the Irish literary renaissance, but he also was the first to impress upon his Anglo-Irish contemporaries that if they were to survive they must somehow come to terms with the Gaelic culture.[4]

Ferguson, though an innovator, was not alone; nor was his approach to the language and literature of Ireland the only route

---

[4] Ferguson was one of the first, if not the first, to use the term 'Anglo-Irish' in a cultural context. In the *Dublin University Magazine* for June 1847, reviewing a life of James Gandon, the English architect who created two of the most splendid public buildings of eighteenth-century Dublin—the Custom House and the Four Courts—Ferguson admitted that Irish architecture of what he called 'the palmy period' belonged to the transplanted civilization of England. But speaking, as he said, 'merely ethnographically', he added this: 'The taste and magnificence which invited them (the English architects) hither, and directed their efforts here, were

to that burdened past. In the early 1840s another young Protestant with a Trinity background. Thomas Davis, began to link the revival of the language with the idea of nationality. His aims were part cultural, part political. In the newspaper, the *Nation*, which he founded with two friends, and in the movement, Young Ireland, which together they launched, Davis drew the outline of an Irish identity that would hardly have been possible before his time. Like Wolfe Tone, he envisaged a future where the different traditions in Ireland would be fused into one, but whereas Wolfe Tone scarcely got beyond asserting that this was what ought to happen, Davis believed that the means for regeneration were primarily cultural and that they could be set to work, provided men realized that time was short and the task urgent. His own time was short indeed, for he died in 1845 aged only 31. Yet in the last three years of his life he propounded a theory of nationality which was to have an enduring influence.

His argument was essentially the same as that of contemporary romantic nationalists on the continent—that the soul of a nation resided in its language. 'A people without a language of its own', he wrote, 'is only half a nation.' 'To lose your native tongue and learn that of an alien, is the worst badge of conquest—it is the chain on the soul. To have lost entirely the national language is death; the fetter has worn through.'[5] To identify the danger was easy, to overcome it more difficult, and Davis did not look for any immediate or mass conversion. Instead, he turned to his own kind, to men of education with the wealth, leisure, and authority to lead. The response never came up to his expectations, but in the generation after his death, to the extent that the flame was kept alive at all, it was tended mainly, though not exclusively, by men of ascendancy background. Of these, two stand out above all others—Standish O'Grady and Douglas Hyde. Both came from

Anglo-Irish' (Lady Ferguson, *Sir Samuel Ferguson in the Ireland of His Day*, i. 291-2). I am indebted for this reference to Dr Maurice Craig, whose *Dublin, 1660-1860* (London, 1952), especially chaps. 15 to 21, explores with great verve and brilliance the process Ferguson was trying to describe.

[5] *Thomas Davis: Essays and Poems with a Centenary Memoir* (Dublin, 1943), pp. 71-2.

Church of Ireland rectories, both had connections with the landed gentry, both were graduates of Trinity College, both retained many of the characteristics of their class, but each made a decisive contribution to the stir and clash of cultures in late nineteenth-century Ireland.

O'Grady was the elder of the two. Born in 1846 and destined apparently for a legal career, he stumbled upon his life's passion almost by accident. As he tells the story, he was marooned in a country house in the west of Ireland on a wet day in the early 1870s. Browsing through an old history of Ireland, he came upon an astonishing fact that nobody had ever mentioned to him before, that his country not only had an ancient past, but that the legends and myths of its pre-history had been embodied in the bardic poetry of the heroic age. So innocent was O'Grady that, although he knew Ferguson socially, he had had no idea that the respected antiquarian was also a poet who had preceded him along this path. However, his 'discovery' sent O'Grady to the Royal Irish Academy and to other sources. From these he pieced together the narrative of the Red Branch or Ulster cycle, and, although ignorant of Irish himself, launched into the two-volume *History of Ireland: The Heroic Period*, which appeared in 1878 and 1880.[6] Some of the material had been used before by Ferguson, but O'Grady brought to it a fire and vividness the older man had never possessed. The *History* did not have a large sale, yet its effect on the rising generation was to be profound. Yeats, Lady Gregory, and other lesser figures all felt the stir of his enthusiasm and each found that he had given them the key to a new world.

O'Grady always remained unrepentantly an ascendancy man, though one so untypical as to earn from Lady Gregory the epithet 'Fenian unionist'. He had little patience with democracy or nationalism and expected the governing class to govern. At the same time, he was well aware that that class had almost missed its hour and he launched appeal after appeal to the gentlemen of Ireland to play their proper part before it was too late. In 1886,

---

[6] He puts the date about 1870, but it was probably several years later. See Philip L. Marcus, *Standish O'Grady* (Bucknell University Press, New Jersey, 1970), p. 14.

much affected both by what he took to be the imminence of Home Rule and also by Lord Randolph Churchill's gospel of Tory Democracy, O'Grady issued an address 'to the landlords of Ireland' in language which they were not accustomed to hear. 'I say', he wrote, 'that even still you are the best class in the country, and for the last two centuries have been; but see, the event proves that you were not good enough, had not virtue enough. Therefore you perish out of the land, while innumerable eyes are dry.' In his heart of hearts O'Grady had little expectation of regenerating them. They were deaf, or blind, he thought, to anything he might say. 'Christ save us all.' he exploded, 'you read nothing, know nothing, This great modern, democratic world rolls on with its thunderings, lightnings, and voices, enough to make the bones of your heroic fathers turn in their graves, and you know nothing about it, care nothing about it.' 'Of you, as a class, as a body of men, I can entertain not the least hope; indeed, who can?'[7] He wrote, therefore, not so much for the class, but for individuals here and there who might still be brands for the saving, and especially for the young 'whose hearts are not yet hardened by contact with the rest or worn out by that grinding attrition'.[8] And them he warned emphatically against the levelling tendencies of the new nationalism which Parnell had brought into being, in terms which may seem to some to have been strangely prophetic:

If you are quite satisfied to lose all that you have inherited, to be stripped naked, and in the slime to wrestle with dragons and gorillas hereafter for some morsel of official income which you will not get, then travel that way. If you are satisfied to see all the worth, virtue, personal refinement, truth, and honour which you know to be inherent in your own order wiped, as with a sponge, out of Ireland—maybe with a bloody sponge—then travel that way. If you wish to see anarchy and civil war, brutal despotisms alternating with bloody lawlessness, or, on the other side, a shabby, sordid Irish Republic, ruled by knavish, corrupt politicians and the ignoble rich, you will travel the way of égalité.[9]

O'Grady here was clearly exhibiting to a marked degree the schizophrenia by which the intelligent minority of the Anglo-Irish was being increasingly affected. He had broken with the

[7] Standish O'Grady, *Selected Essays and Passages* (London, n.d.), pp. 221–2, 224.
[8] Ibid., p. 226.
[9] Ibid., pp. 227–8.

traditional concerns of his class, just as his exact contemporary, Parnell, had broken with them too. But whereas Parnell, by espousing the land agitation, had struck at the economic base of landlordism and had turned his face towards the creation of a self-governing Ireland in which the middle class, though led by him, would be dominant, O'Grady, bitterly though he condemned his peers, disliked even more bitterly the prospect of democratic mediocrity which he saw ahead. For him, the future lay in the gentlemen of Ireland identifying themselves with the country both in its culture and in its economy. Like Yeats a little later, he could perceive a natural affinity between squire and peasant, since the enemy of both was modern commerce and all its attendant vulgarity.

One of the young men whom O'Grady influenced, but whose very different evolution helps to emphasize the cultural fluidity of these critical decades, was Douglas Hyde. Hyde was born in 1860 and educated at home at Frenchpark, county Roscommon, where his irascible father was rector. Being educated at home meant, among other things, constant contact with country people who still used Irish as their ordinary spoken tongue. Because they were unlettered, they had preserved much of the oral tradition of the west of Ireland and from them Hyde picked up not only the language, but the poetry and folk-lore of an Ireland closed to nearly all his contemporaries. Then in 1880 he went to Trinity, whence he graduated with high honours in modern literature four years later. During that period he mingled with the scholars of the Royal Irish Academy and with the brilliant young men—T. W. Rolleston and Charles Oldham the chief of them—who had also recently graduated from Trinity and who in 1885 launched the *Dublin University Review* to fill the gap left by the cessation of the *Dublin University Magazine* in 1877. These young men represented a striking deviation from the traditional Anglo-Irish culture. Although the products of Trinity, they were not congealed within the austere Anglican-unionist ethos which the university establishment rigorously maintained. On the contrary, they were conscious of movement towards some as yet undefined goal; their minds were open and hopeful for the future.

They did not, however, share a common political standpoint and both in the *Review* and in the Contemporary Club which Oldham also founded in 1885 (just across the road from the front gate of Trinity), nationalists and unionists argued endlessly but amicably. Hyde was emphatically a nationalist, indeed a republican sympathizer at this time, though in his adult life and work he was always to keep politics at arm's length. But more than anything, he was a real Irish speaker and writer in a circle where approval of the language was a good deal more articulate than performance in it. His first Irish poems were written while he was in his teens and he adopted his famous pseudonym, An Craoibhín Aoibhinn (The Pleasant Little Branch), even before he went to Trinity. Soon he was so well known that in 1886 the *Review* could ask editorially what it was that Hyde and his friends really wanted of Irish. Was it to make it the language of conversation and the newspapers? Was it to make Ireland a bilingual country? Or was there to be a virtual separation between Irish-speaking Ireland and English-speaking Ireland? And might it not be best, in fact, to treat Irish as a classical language and leave it to the universities?

This provoked from Hyde 'A Plea for the Irish Language' which was an important milestone in his evolution and in that of the whole Gaelic revival. It was not, he admitted, his aim to make Irish the language of everyday speech and communication, 'because that is and ever shall be an impossibility'. But it might at least be possible, if not to spread it (which he doubted), at least to prevent it from dying out. The time was to come when the policy of 'preservation' of the existing Irish-speaking area, the Gaeltacht, versus the policy of 'revival' over the country at large, would produce a major conflict in the movement, but for the moment Hyde was concerned to make the same point as Davis forty years earlier—that language was an essential part of nationality and that for it to disappear altogether would be a kind of death. He summed up his position thus:

In conclusion may we say this, that while our social and commercial relations make it a necessity for every man, woman and child in this kingdom to learn English sooner or later, reverence for our past history, regard for the memory of our ancestors, our national honour, and the fear of becoming materialised and losing our best and highest characteristics call upon us imperatively to assist the Irish-speaking population at the present crisis and to establish for all time a bilingual population in those parts of Ireland where Irish is now spoken, from whom all those who in the distant future may wish to investigate the history or the antiquities of our nation may draw as from a fountain that vernacular knowledge which for such purpose is indispensably necessary.[10]

Both in the *Review* and in the Contemporary Club two tendencies were becoming increasingly obvious. On the one hand, it was clear that a number of the young Trinity-bred intellectuals had been powerfully excited by the rise of an effective nationalism under Parnell. On the other hand, it was equally clear that their new nationalism was refreshingly non-sectarian. Taken together, these two tendencies seemed to point towards a fusion of cultures, and in this incipient fusion one man was to be of particular importance. This was John O'Leary. O'Leary was a Catholic who had been educated at Trinity, had learned his nationalism from Davis and Young Ireland and had then become prominent in the Fenian movement of the 1860s. Arrested when the government broke up that conspiracy, he served a term in prison, was exiled for a longer period in France, but returned to Ireland in 1885. The young men and women whose imaginations had been aroused by romantic nationalism gathered round him eagerly and he was to influence profoundly a whole generation. A man of striking appearance and stoic courage, he had little time for conventional politics, or for land agitation, or for surreptitious violence. He stood for a republic which would have to be fought for in the open field eventually. But that time was not yet, and meanwhile he encouraged his disciples to immerse themselves in the Irish past and to recover from oblivion the history and literature of their nation.

The most important of O'Leary's conquests was W. B. Yeats. Yeats was then in his early twenties and his first serious work had begun to appear in the *Dublin University Review*. Under O'Leary's influence he turned away from Pre-Raphaelite temptations and his poetry increasingly concerned itself with Irish themes. In 1888 he collaborated with Douglas Hyde in an anthology of the poetry

[10] Cited in Dominic Daly, *The Young Douglas Hyde* (Dublin, 1974), p. 68.

of Young Ireland and in rapid succession produced several
volumes of Irish fairy and folk tales. Then in 1890 occurred the
violent convulsion caused by Parnell's involvement in the O'Shea
divorce case. The Irish party, under pressure both from English
Liberalism and Irish Catholicism to choose between their leader
and Home Rule, broke in two. A majority declared against
Parnell, but he refused to capitulate and in the eleven months of
life that remained to him fought a frenzied campaign for survival
until his sudden death in October 1891 at the age of 45. The split
in the Irish party was not healed, but continued with extreme
bitterness for another nine years.

This shattering end to the high hopes of the 1880s produced in
the new generation a revulsion from the constitutional politics to
which Parnell had given shape and style and purpose. That
revulsion provided the opportunity for nationalism to become, for
a time at least, cultural rather than political. Literature, as the
main channel of this cultural nationalism, began to seem suddenly
more central, more relevant. It was no longer, as Dr John Kelly
has truly observed, merely to be regarded as 'ornamentation', but,
and this in a highly chauvinistic way, as 'an essential part of the
national identity'.[11] In that sense Yeats was quite right in saying
that a new spirit came into Ireland with the fall of the leader and
that this opened the way for a whole series of transformations. In
some of these Yeats himself took a major part. Parnell was barely
two months dead when in December 1891 Yeats, with T. W.
Rolleston, launched the Irish Literary Society of London, following this by the creation in Dublin, in May 1892 and with O'Leary's
help, of the National Literary Society. The principal aim of both
bodies was to publicize the literature, legends, and folk-lore of
Ireland. Caught up in his own enthusiasm, Yeats bubbled over
with projects—for small branch lending libraries throughout the
country, for a travelling theatre, for the re-publication of various
works of Irish history and literature.

We need not pursue these enterprises, for they mostly foun-
dered. But the reason for their foundering is important because it

[11] John Kelly, 'The Fall of Parnell and the Rise of Irish Literature: an Interpretation', in *Anglo-Irish Studies*, ii. 1–23 (1976).

is directly connected with the clash of cultures which was to fill the first decade of the new century with its clangour. When it came to choosing books for publication or for stocking the libraries, Yeats found himself surrounded by the devotees of Young Ireland, who wished to perpetuate what Yeats, with his unwavering critical judgement, knew to be good propaganda but bad literature. His purpose was to create a new literary movement, which would indeed use Irish themes from the past, but which would not be content with simply embalming what had been handed on by previous generations. Yet, though he fought furiously, he was beaten down and had the first of many lessons in the power of conservatism in nationalist Ireland.

But the argument between Yeats and his opponents went deeper than a conflict between art and propaganda. It concerned also the question of language as the symbol of cultural difference. Although as attracted as anyone by the material for poetry and drama which legend and folklore had revealed, Yeats had virtually no Irish. But even had he managed to learn it, this would not have affected his ambition, which was to create a literature that would not be merely local, but would have a European impact; it would, therefore, inevitably be a literature in English. And because those who would produce it must write out of their own experience, and not merely serve as ventriloquists' dummies for Young Ireland, the most urgent need was for the 'de-Davisization' of Irish literature. The phrase was actually invented by a school-fellow of Yeats's, the librarian W. K. Magee, who, under the pseudonym John Eglinton, wrote often and pungently in defence of the Anglo-Irish culture, but the actual burden of de-Davisization was to fall mainly on Yeats in the years ahead.

There was, however, another way of looking at the problem, which was to say that what Ireland needed was not de-Davisization, but de-Anglicization. This was pre-eminently the view of Douglas Hyde, but he was not alone in taking it. As far back as 1884, a small group of men meeting in the Tipperary town of Thurles had founded the Gaelic Athletic Association. Their purpose was to revive Irish sports—hurling and, later, the Gaelic version of football—and after slow beginnings they had such

success that to this day the hurling and Gaelic football champion-
ships inspire in the Irish counties passionate loyalties and enthusi-
asms. The drive behind the Association went far beyond the
merely athletic. As the new movement's sponsor, the Roman
Catholic Archbishop of Cashel, Dr Croke, declared, the widespread adoption of English games was only a part of the betrayal
of the national heritage. 'If we continue', he said, 'travelling for
the next score years in the same direction that we have been
going in for some time past . . . effacing our national features as
though we were ashamed of them, and putting on, with England's
stuffs and broadcloths her masher habits, and other such effemi-
nate follies as she may recommend, we had better at once, and
publicly, abjure our nationality.'[12]

Not to abjure, but to express that nationality, both in Irish
verse and in translations from the Irish, was Douglas Hyde's
ambition. In 1889 and 1890 he published two volumes in Irish,
but it was the appearance in 1893 of his *Love Songs of Connacht*, in
Irish and English, that marked, as Yeats truly said, 'the coming of
a new power into literature'. With extraordinary delicacy and
fidelity, Hyde had managed to convey Gaelic rhythms and turns
of speech into an English which was marvellously transformed
thereby. One out of many of his translations may, even without
the Irish original, illustrate what I mean. It is from a song he was
given by an old woman living in a hut in a bog. Here it is both in
his literal translation and in the verses he made therefrom. The
literal translation is as follows:[13]

My Grief on the Sea

My grief on the sea, it is that it is big. It is it that is going between me and my
thousand treasures. I was left at home making grief, without any hope of going
over sea with me, for ever or for aye. My grief that I am not, and my white
múirnín, in the province of Leinster or County of Clare. My sorrow I am not,
and my thousand loves, on board of a ship voyaging to America. A bed of
rushes was under me last night, and I threw it out with the heat of the day.
My love came to my side, shoulder to shoulder and mouth on mouth.

[12] T. F. O'Sullivan, *The Story of the G.A.A.* (Dublin, 1916), pp. 9–10.
[13] Douglas Hyde, *The Love Songs of Connacht* (Dublin, Dun Emer Press edn.,
1904), pp. 20–1, 107–8.

Although Yeats preferred this version as being nearer to 'that beautiful English of the country people who remember too much Irish to talk like a newspaper', Hyde's verse translation has its own magic:

> My grief on the sea,
> How the waves of it roll!
> For they heave between me
> And the love of my soul!
>
> Abandoned, forsaken,
> To grief and to care,
> Will the sea ever waken
> Relief from despair?
>
> My grief and my trouble!
> Would he and I were
> In the province of Leinster,
> Or county of Clare.
>
> Were I and my darling—
> Oh, heart-bitter wound!—
> On board of the ship
> For America bound.
>
> On a green bed of rushes
> All last night I lay,
> And I flung it abroad
> With the heat of the day.
>
> And my love came behind me—
> He came from the South;
> His breast to my bosom,
> His mouth to my mouth.

Synge, Lady Gregory, and Yeats were all affected by Hyde, yet his aim remained fundamentally different from theirs. For him, his English translations were incidental to his main work, which

was to create, or re-create, a literature in Irish. He was emphatic
that this had to be done urgently, for a reason which he explained
in 1892 in a lecture that became famous—'The Necessity for De-
Anglicising Ireland'. This was in effect a restatement in terms of
the 1890s of what Davis had said in the 1840s, though, as Hyde
well knew, the prospects for an Irish revival had become much
worse in the intervening fifty years. Hyde protested not so much
against imitating the best of English culture, but rather against the
slavish conformism which made the Irish adopt everything
English simply because it was English. How illogical it was, he
said, to condemn English domination, as many did, and yet to
discard the one thing that distinguished the Irish from their
masters—the language:

It has always been very curious to me how Irish sentiment sticks in this half-way
house—how it continues to apparently hate the English and at the same time
continues to imitate them; how it continues to clamour for recognition as a
distinct nationality, and at the same time throws away with both hands what
would make it so.[14]

How, Hyde asked, could the Irish hope to produce anything of
value in art, literature or institutions if they persisted in cherishing
this inner contradiction? His anwer was that only by strenuous
efforts to revive and restore Irish as a living language and a living
literature could a separate identity for the country be preserved.
Irish names, Irish sports, Irish music, even Irish clothes, all must
be brought back into daily use. At the same time a strong
counter-current must be created against English goods, English
habits, English ideas, for the pressure of the dominant culture
was so strong that, unless strenuously resisted, it would overwhelm
them like a flood. 'We will become what, I fear, we are largely at
present, a nation of imitators, the Japanese of Western Europe,
lost to the power of native initiative and alive only to second-hand
assimilation.'[15]

It was not long before Hyde's teaching began to produce results.
One of those who learnt from him was a young civil servant from

[14] Douglas Hyde, 'The Necessity for De-Anglicising Ireland', in Sir Charles
Gavan Duffy, George Sigerson, and Douglas Hyde, *The Revival of Irish Literature*
(London, 1894), p. 117.
[15] Ibid., p. 119.

Antrim, Eoin MacNeill. In March 1893 MacNeill published 'A Plea and a Plan for the Extension of the Movement to Preserve and Spread the Irish Language' and followed this up shortly afterwards by calling a few enthusiasts together to form a new organization for that purpose, the Gaelic League.[16] MacNeill was an Ulster Catholic and those whom he summoned to his meeting included two Catholic priests (Father Eugene O'Growney and Father Michael O'Hickey), as well as Douglas Hyde and several other Protestants. It is evident, therefore, that the new organization was conceived at the outset as a means of bringing together representatives of different cultures who had the same aim in mind. From about the turn of the century Protestant participation is said to have declined. If it did, this was probably because the connection between 'Gaelicism' and nationalism was becoming more overt and the decision of the Gaelic League in 1900 not to become involved with the Pan-Celtic movement may have been a pointer in this direction. When Hyde was elected president he bent all his efforts towards ensuring that the League should be non-political. He remained president from 1893 until 1915 and only resigned then when it became impossible at that tense time to exclude politics any longer. During its formative years the League had, as its founders intended, been primarily a vehicle for the revival of Irish as a spoken and a written language. Yet for many, and in a sense for Hyde himself, to say that it should be educational and not political was a meaningless distinction. It was indeed desirable that the League should not be linked with any one party or any one programme, since this would deprive it of its universality. But events were to show that most of the young men and women who brought the old militancy back into politics in the first two decades of the twentieth century had begun their apprenticeship inside the Gaelic League. It could hardly have been otherwise, since the central gospel of the League was that the revival of the national language was the essential condition for the revival of the national sense of identity.

[16] *Gaelic Journal*, 6 Mar. 1893, reprinted in F. X. Martin and F. J. Byrne (ed.), *The Scholar Revolutionary: Eoin MacNeill, 1867–1945 and the Making of the New Ireland* (Shannon, Ireland, 1973), appendix 2, pp. 357–63.

What was at stake here, as Hyde and the other founders of the League fully realized, was, as one contemporary phrased it, 'a battle of two civilisations'.[17] But it was an uneven battle. The logic of a language revival was that Ireland should become what it had not been for more than a century, a predominantly Irish-speaking country. To achieve this again the Gaeltacht would have needed cherishing and reinvigorating by a variety of educational, social, and economic measures which themselves would have been political acts, but which the League, by its deliberate abstention from politics, had debarred itself from initiating. Yet, even if the League had been able to commit itself to such an ambitious programme, lack of means would almost certainly have defeated it. The problem of resuscitating Irish had become so complex that state intervention on a large scale would have been needed if there was to be any chance of success. And given the many failures of state intervention after 1921 in the much more favourable circumstances created by the winning of political independence, it is hard to believe that the British government, in the unlikely event of it having been willing to experiment in that direction before 1914, would have been more effective.[18] Not surprisingly, the League grew slowly, and the Gaeltacht, so far from growing, continued steadily to diminish. After four years of hard work by its founders only 43 branches of the League had been formed, though with improved teaching facilities and techniques of promotion, the pace quickened in the new century and by 1904 nearly 600 branches were in existence. The outward signs that something unusual and far-reaching was happening were the official recognition in 1904 of the League's campaign for bi-lingualism in primary schools in Irish-speaking areas, and, still more striking, the decision of the National University of Ireland (established in 1908) to include Irish as a compulsory subject for matriculation.

All this certainly testified to the resilience of the old Gaelic culture in its modern form, but it remained nevertheless the

---

[17] D. P. Moran, *The Philosophy of Irish Ireland* (Dublin, 1905), see especially chap. 6.
[18] For the post-1921 situation, see lecture 6 below.

culture of a minority, even though of an intelligent and ultimately influential minority. Perhaps, after all, the League's most remarkable achievement was to establish in the imagination of some of the most ardent spirits of the new century a sense of shared endeavour in the restoration of life to something precious that had come close to extinction. The first fumbling steps in obscure class-rooms to master 'O'Growney', the summer expeditions to the teaching colleges which the League set up in the Gaeltacht and elsewhere, the dancing and singing and music, and always the hard grind at the language—these produced in that idealistic and earnestly self-improving generation before the First World War a dedication to an Ireland liberated from the pressures of a foreign culture, which was to have an importance for the country far beyond its significance for the happy few who felt it bliss in that dawn to be alive.[19]

Yet, if the Gaelic League was a unifying influence, it was also a divisive one, for it helped to precipitate, and indeed to define, the emerging conflict between Irish Ireland and Anglo-Irish Ireland. It is aptly symbolic that one of the first indications of that conflict should have been the increasing isolation of Trinity College on the central issue of the future of the Irish language. In 1899 a commission enquired into the lowly status of Irish in the secondary schools. Amongst those who gave evidence were the Professor of Sanskrit and Comparative Philology in Trinity, an English-born scholar named Robert Atkinson; J. P. Mahaffy, then a Senior Fellow of the College; and Douglas Hyde. The attitude of Atkinson and Mahaffy was contemptuous in the extreme. Atkinson told the commission that in ancient Irish literature 'it would be difficult to find a book in which there is not some passage so silly or indecent as to give you a shock from which you would not recover for the rest of your life'. Most of it, he thought, was folklore and 'all folklore was at bottom abominable'. Mahaffy, though he once described Atkinson as a brilliant

[19] For the progress and role of the Gaelic League, see D. Greene, 'The Founding of the Gaelic League', in S. Ó Tuama (ed.), *The Gaelic League Idea* (Cork and Dublin, 1972), pp. 9–19, and T. Ó hÁilín, 'Irish revival movements', in B. Ó Cuív (ed.), *A View of the Irish Language* (Dublin, 1969), pp. 91–100.

linguist who knew the language of every European country save the one he happened to be in, was not above using him as an expert on Irish; indeed, he had to, for he had no Irish himself. He therefore followed suit, condemning the Irish text-books then in use as either silly or indecent, or else religious. The subject, he said, was of no practical use to school children, though he admitted that when fishing or shooting in the west, he had himself found a few phrases serviceable. If there must be an emphasis on the native language, he suggested 'that beautiful pre-Gaelic speech of which only three words remain. Anyone with a little aptitude can learn them in a week.'[20]

There is an arrogant frivolity about these *obiter dicta* that reminds us of the brutal aspect of the ascendancy culture which the Trinity of that day, with its strange mixture of brilliant scholarship and savage, internal vendettas, exemplified to the full. Usually, the dons kept their way, oblivious to the currents that had drawn so many of their promising young men into a world of new ideas and outlandish objectives; and usually the young men let them go, torn between affection for their eccentricity, respect for their learning, and aversion from their politics. But this time the affront was too direct and touched too sensitive a nerve. A storm of protest rained down upon Mahaffy and Atkinson, but the most effective criticism was that embodied by Douglas Hyde in an article entitled 'A University Scandal'. Hyde wrote from the strong position of a graduate who loved his university and was moved more to sorrow than to anger by the grotesque antics of those whom he had been brought up to revere. Perhaps also he was human enough to resent the fact that a few years earlier Atkinson had blocked his appointment to a professorship of Irish in Trinity. At any rate, he had no difficulty in showing that Mahaffy was entirely ignorant of the language he traduced, and that Atkinson, though a respectable philologist, had no competence in Irish literature. The real reason for their hostility, he shrewdly suggested, was an instinctive fear that the language movement would reinforce the separatist movement and thus threaten their favoured position in an Ireland still dominated

[20] W. B. Stanford and R. B. McDowell, *Mahaffy* (London, 1971), chap. 6.

intellectually by the ascendancy. To Hyde the blind folly which dictated this intransigence was deeply shocking. 'How I wish', he exclaimed, 'that Trinity College would not thrust herself forward as the undying opponent of all things Irish . . . How I wish that he and his colleagues would recognise the fact that a new intellectual Ireland has arisen and strive to place their university *en rapport* with it.'[21]

That Trinity should find itself at odds with the new intellectual Ireland was predictable enough, but Hyde's campaign for the language had other and more serious consequences. Not only did it drive a wedge between him and Yeats, who mourned in the Gaelic Leaguer 'the great poet that had died in his [Hyde's] youth', but it made it more explicit the contradiction that lay at the heart of the literary movement. For Yeats and his friends, it cannot be too often repeated, the true ambition was to create an Irish literature in English, which would take its place as a part of European civilization. But for Hyde and *his* friends, though art was not negligible, far more important was the propaganda for cultural nationalism which the Gaelic League existed to promote. The breach between the two men, and between the two cultures, was not to become absolute for a few years yet, but with the next stage in the developing conflict, the foundation of the Irish National Theatre, the common ground they had hitherto shared began rapidly to diminish.

The history of the movement which led first to the creation of an Irish Literary Theatre and ultimately to the establishment of the Abbey Theatre is well-trodden ground which we do not need to traverse in detail. Its significance for our present purposes is that it brought together the key figures of the literary renaissance and that these, though differing in religious and social backgrounds, were without exception representatives of the Anglo-Irish culture. Not all of them agreed about how their theatre should develop and not all of them stayed with it after the first raptures had worn off. But between 1897 and 1900 the combined forces of the four

[21] Douglas Hyde, 'A University Scandal', in *New Ireland Review* (Dec. 1889), p. 204; Gareth W. Dunleavy, *Douglas Hyde* (Bucknell University Press, New Jersey, 1974), pp. 38–9.

founders—Yeats, Lady Gregory, George Moore, and Edward Martyn—brought the theatre into being, and provided it with its first plays. Many influences, as has often been pointed out, went to the making of this experiment. In part a reaction against the commercial theatre of London, in part an imitation of the art theatre of Paris, it owed more in its beginnings to the fact that its begetters were literary artists than to any real knowledge of the drama, of which only George Moore had a smattering. It was influenced to some extent by Ibsen, still more by Wagner, but most of all by the sources which lay nearest to hand—the heroic legends of the Irish past and the folklore which could still be gathered in the Irish countryside. Above all it was an attempt, of which Yeats was the most articulate exponent, to achieve through the theatre a sense of nationality which would transcend purely political values because it would restore to the nation its soul. 'We will show', said the fund-raising prospectus of the movement, 'that Ireland is not the home of buffoonery and of easy sentiment, as it has been represented, but the home of an ancient idealism.'[22]

The collaborators Yeats gathered about him were an incongruous trio. George Moore, easily the best known of them, was also the most marginal. Of Catholic landlord stock, in this, as in all things, he refused to conform to type, being both a lapsed Catholic and an absentee landlord. His reputation as a novelist was at its height, and it was as a novelist that he viewed the theatre movement, which in due course yielded him material for some of the funniest pages of his comic masterpiece, *Hail and Farewell*. Edward Martyn, his distant relation, was also a Catholic (a devout one), and in his family peasant and aristocratic strains were mingled. A Galway landlord who lived only a couple of miles from Lady Gregory's house, Coole Park, he was a wealthy man who combined personal austerity with lavish generosity to the arts. He was an ardent Ibsenite and hoped—in vain, as it turned out—that the new theatre would bring to Ireland a cosmopolitan drama braced by the keen air of Scandinavia. Lady Gregory, ultimately the most influential of the three, was at the outset the

[22] Lady Gregory, *Our Irish Theatre* (Gerrard's Cross, 1972 edn.), p. 20.

greatest tyro. Though notable in her neighbourhood for her care of her tenants, and beginning to develop what must have seemed to them an eccentric interest in their vernacular Irish, she had not yet found an outlet for the intellectual energy and organizing ability pent up within her since her husband's death a few years earlier.

As for Yeats himself, he was at this time a prey to many conflicting influences. From John O'Leary he was absorbing, as we have seen, a lofty view of his duty to Ireland, though he was at the same time becoming critical of the arid abstractions of the Young Ireland gospel which his mentor still revered. At the same time, his passionate and hopeless love for Maud Gonne led him in her wake into the vacuous politics of extremism. Intermingled with these preoccupations was his abiding obsession with the occult. This he sought to share with Maud Gonne and was in all seriousness planning with her to create an Irish mystical order (in which he also tried to interest Douglas Hyde) with its headquarters in a ruined castle on an island in Loch Key on the borders of Sligo and Roscommon. Neither the order nor its headquarters materialized, but to Yeats—or at least to one part of him—the theatre represented an alternative means of expressing the magical and mystical ideas which underlay all his work at this time. But it also represented something more. In later years he was to recall that when he was 23 or 24 one sentence had formed itself in his mind: 'Hammer your thoughts into unity'.[23] It was a sentence that haunted him all his life, though he defined it at different times in different terms, sometimes as 'Unity of Being', sometimes as 'Unity of Culture'. Unity of Culture was to the social group what Unity of Being was to the individual. In the theatre he saw the means of forging a Unity of Culture for Ireland. A nation, he maintained, could not exist if there were 'no national institutions to reverence, no national success to admire, without a model of it in the mind of the people'.[24] As in ancient Greece, so in modern Ireland, the drama would be the means of projecting art into life, and so of providing Ireland with 'a vision of the race

[23] W. B. Yeats, *Explorations* (London, 1962), p. 263. This phrase begins the essay, 'If I were Four-and-Twenty', first published in 1919.

[24] W. B. Yeats, *Autobiographies* (London, 1955), p. 493, from a diary kept in 1909.

as noble as that of Sophocles and of Aeschylus'. And yet, as he admitted, since the Irish people were 'not educated enough to accept images more profound, more true to human nature, than the schoolboy thoughts of Young Ireland', the vision he sought to create would be sure to be attacked by those who preferred Young Ireland rhetoric or even 'the obvious sentiment of popular English literature'.[25]

When he wrote those words in 1909 Yeats was looking back upon the great battles he had fought on behalf of J. M. Synge, and at which we must glance in the next lecture, but some of the opprobrium and misunderstanding which Synge's work attracted had begun to manifest itself much earlier, indeed almost from the beginning of the new theatre's career. The plays with which it opened in May 1899 might almost have been chosen for the express purpose of illustrating the ambivalence of the new move-ment. One was Edward Martyn's *The Heather Field*, a five-finger exercise avowedly on the Ibsenite model. The other was Yeats's *The Countess Cathleen*, which, like *The Heather Field*, had been published some years before. *The Countess Cathleen*, an early example of Yeats in his aristocratic mood, recounts the story of a great lady who in time of famine is prepared to sell her soul to the devil that her people may have food. This, which did not accord with the conventional view of Irish piety, was attacked before the play was even staged, most notoriously in a pamphlet, *Souls for Gold*, by F. H. O'Donnell, a discredited politician. Rumours of clerical disapproval brought Martyn almost to the point of with-drawing his financial backing and he was only placated when Yeats resourcefully produced two ecclesiastical opinions in its favour. Notwithstanding this precaution, the reception of the play was stormy, prefiguring other and larger quarrels still to come. Among its vociferous opponents were some students of the Catholic University College, who followed their demonstration in the theatre by a letter of protest to the press, against an art 'which offers as a type of our people a loathsome brood of apostates'.[26] They were not unanimous, however. One at least

[25] Ibid., p. 494.
[26] *Freeman's Journal*, 10 May 1889.

among them applauded the play on its first night and refused to sign the protest. He was James Joyce who thus, in his first year at the university, took the lonely road of artistic independence.[27]

The new venture fared better with the critics than with the students and the Irish Literary Theatre established itself sufficiently to complete the three-year experiment envisaged by its founders, and even, in its third season, to mount Douglas Hyde's *Casadh an tSúgán* (*The Twisting of the Rope*), the first play in Irish ever to be presented by a Dublin theatre. By that time, as we shall see in the next lecture, Yeats was preparing to take the theatre in a wholly different direction. For the moment we may leave it with certain questions unanswered, questions posed by F. H. O'Donnell in his pamphlet. 'What is the meaning of this rubbish? How is it to help the national cause? How is it to help any cause at all?'[28] Here, crudely stated, was an attitude of mind that Yeats and his friends were constantly to encounter in the years ahead. A theatre, or a play, or a book, or a poem that claimed to be 'national' would be judged according to whether or not it conformed to the stereotype which ascribed to Catholic Ireland the virtues of purity, innocence, and sanctity. To impugn those virtues, to ignore the stereotype, to disdain propaganda, and instead to say of literature, as Yeats did, that it 'must take the responsibility of its power and keep all its freedom', and on that basis to seek to forge a unity of culture, was to make certain assumptions about the nature of society which were justified by nothing in the Irish experience.[29]

Yet, as the century closed, voices such as O'Donnell's might have seemed no more than a tiresome and anachronistic echo from a vanished past. The real Ireland seemed to be growing more peaceful, more prosperous, even more united. Here, too, Parnell's end had seemed to mark a new beginning. While the politicians squabbled, successive governments showered reforms on Ireland—stimulating land purchase, founding the Congested

[27] Richard Ellmann, *James Joyce* (New York, 1959), pp. 68–9.

[28] F. H. O'Donnell, *Souls for Gold: Pseudo-Celtic Drama* (London, 1899), in W. A. Henderson Press Cuttings (N.L.I. MS. 1729), p. 325.

[29] W. B. Yeats, *Explorations*, p. 117, from the essay, 'The Irish Dramatic Movement', published in the occasional magazine *Samhain*, 1903.

Districts Board to relieve the poverty of the west, conceding elective local government, establishing a Department of Agriculture and Technical Instruction. These new departures were important, but their impact on the Irish countryside was necessarily gradual. The life lived in that countryside by the farmers and labourers and their families remained arduous and in some ways primitive. There were few comforts in their houses and few amenities in the market-towns that served them. The demographic pattern established since the Famine dictated the unusual combination of late marriages, large families, and many unmarried sons and daughters. This was a recipe for conservatism, and the Irish peasant, conditioned by his history to attach more importance to the tenure of land than to its use, and fortified in his social attitudes by his Church, was a very conservative person indeed.

Yet, if the fashionable doctrine of nationality was ever to rise above mere rhetoric, some means must be found for creating tolerable living conditions and a sound economic base for Irish rural society. A new initiative was needed, and once again it was to be an Anglo-Irish initiative, taken by a man who did as much as anyone, except perhaps Yeats and Lady Gregory, to bridge the gulf between the cultures. This was Sir Horace Plunkett. Born in 1854 of an old landed family with Catholic branches as well as the Protestant one to which he belonged, Plunkett had been educated at Eton and Oxford and then, under threat of tuberculosis, had spent ten years ranching in America. From 1889 onwards, he divided his life between estate and business interests in England and Ireland, but being a wealthy and energetic bachelor, he still found the time to turn his attention to Irish agriculture and its practitioners.

The panacea he advocated, and to which he devoted some of the best years of his life, was agricultural co-operation. Strongly influenced by the Danish experience, he wanted to use co-operation not just to lead Irish farmers towards a more efficient use of their land and stock, but to regenerate a people, naturally cheerful and friendly, but, as he thought, soured and embittered by obsessive concern with politics and religion. At the start he concentrated on the dairying industry, with the object of improving the quality of Irish butter and cheese, and though he set up the first of his dairies, or 'creameries' as they are still called in Ireland, in 1889, it was ominous that he had to address more than forty meetings before he could overcome the suspicion and timidity of the local farmers, to say nothing of the jealousy of priests and curates, resentful of any encroachment upon their traditional spheres of authority. Gradually, he began to gather allies—from his own class, Lord Monteagle; a young land-agent, R. A. Anderson; the Jesuit, Father Tom Finlay; and, above all, George William Russell, known to posterity by his pseudonym, AE. Russell was a northern Protestant, born at Lurgan in 1867. He came to Dublin in his youth to study art (Yeats was one of his fellow-students), but had to earn his living as a clerk in a Dublin drapery store. He was a mystic, an indifferent poet and painter, a superb journalist, an original thinker on social problems, a fosterer of young talent, a man of courage who for nearly half a century was to stand at the centre of the country's cultural and intellectual life.

Russell joined the co-operative movement as a travelling organizer in 1897. By then progress had been such that Plunkett had been able to establish a national base in the Irish Agricultural Organisation Society and had followed this by launching a co-operative journal, *The Irish Homestead*. When AE took over the editorship, the paper rapidly became a cultural as well as an agricultural force, preaching always that gospel of co-operation in the widest sense which lay at the heart of Plunkett's idealism.

There was, of course, a limit to what one man could do in his private capacity and in 1892 Plunkett entered politics as an extremely independent unionist to win public support for his aims. Up to a point he succeeded, and the establishment of the Department of Agriculture and Technical Instruction, of which he was the first head, was largely the fruit of his enterprise in organizing some unionists and some nationalists (though by no means all of either persuasion) to press for government aid for Irish agriculture. It was Plunkett, also, who was one of the sponsors of the All Ireland Committee of 1897, where all shades of Irish opinion came together to denounce the over-taxation of Ireland to which a recent report had drawn attention. It proved impossible, however, to agree upon a formula requesting the government to redress the situation and the strange spectacle of unionist and nationalist combining against English 'oppression' was seen no more. To Standish O'Grady this failure to exploit a unique opportunity was but further evidence of what he called 'the Great Enchantment' which brooded like a poisonous fog over the land, 'paralysing the understandings of the wise, melting to water the hearts of the brave'.[30]

The truth was less melodramatic and more complicated. In Ireland it is always necessary to distinguish between what appears on the surface and the currents which eddy underneath. Superficially, it seemed, as the nineteenth century ended, that a new era was opening, an era of constructive thinking and doing in which men and women of different cultures might join in friendly collaboration. In literature and drama, in economic and social improvement, in private initiatives and through official agencies, a truly united Ireland looked to be on the verge of creation. It did indeed appear that the fall and death of Parnell had released talents and energies from bondage to politics which could now be employed in building a better society. No one can turn over the newspapers and periodicals, or read the public records and the private memoirs, without sensing the intense intellectual ferment which filled the country, and more particularly Dublin, at that time.

And yet those currents still eddied underneath. We shall best understand their significance if we think again of the four cultures which I mentioned in my first lecture. Leaving aside for the present the Presbyterian-dominated culture of the north-east, which did not much impinge on the rest of the country, we can say that two of the other cultures, the Anglo-Irish and the Gaelic, were now in active revolt against the English. The English culture was still so dominant that its exponents could go through life almost unaware of the other cultures, whose protagonists, though highly articulate, were always few in numbers. But these two

[30] Standish O'Grady, *Selected Essays and Passages*, p. 176.

other cultures, while apparently sharing similar aims, were so different in outlook and intent that much of the conflict in the coming years was to arise out of the quarrel that soon developed between them. In essence, it was the quarrel between an Irish Ireland, which insisted that all who were not with it were against it, and an Anglo-Irish Ireland, which fought desperately to establish a common ground between the Gaelic and the English cultures and to call that common ground simply 'Irish'.

Out of all this excitement and conflict anything might have come. What did come was extraordinary achievement, combined with extraordinary bitterness. In my next lecture I want to lay the achievement and the bitterness side by side and in doing so to try not only to discover why the high hopes so many people held at the turn of the century had vanished only a dozen years later, but also to point forward towards the crucial change of emphasis which began to be apparent around 1912 and which ushered in the revolutionary decade that obliterated so much of the old Ireland. We shall be passing, then, from a phase of fusion and co-operation, when everything seemed possible, to a phase dominated by 'the battle of two civilizations', when the fissures in Irish society reappeared, deeper and more unbridgeable than ever.

3

Irish Ireland versus Anglo-Irish Ireland

THE attempt to bring about a fusion of cultures which I described in my last lecture was based on three implicit assumptions. One was that in achieving this goal the Anglo-Irish had a special part to play: educated, leisured, self-confident, they would, in this sphere as in others, naturally take the lead. The second assumption was that there was a broad area of common ground between Irish Ireland and Anglo-Irish Ireland on which increasing collaboration could be built. And the third and most far-reaching assumption was that cultural fusion and regeneration were the agreed objectives of a society which had laid aside its political differences.

None of these assumptions ever won general acceptance. On the contrary, the great interest of the first decade of the new century is to see how fusion was first resisted, and then destroyed, by hostile forces. Essentially, they were the forces of resurgent nationalism, allied with a still powerful and articulate Catholicism. Operating from a different concept of unity from that of the Anglo-Irish, they could admit no resting-place between the rejection of the English culture and the restoration of the Gaelic culture. We have seen already the obstacles Yeats had encountered in his struggle to break free from the shackles of Young Ireland and Horace Plunkett's difficulties in overcoming the suspicions of priests and small farmers when launching his co-operative experiment. Now we have to watch the same battle being fought out in a larger arena and with a much more acute awareness on both sides of the issues at stake.

Among nationalists this greater awareness was due partly to the rise of a new movement and partly to the publication of a new

journal. The new movement was Sinn Féin, the new journal was
the weekly periodical, *The Leader*, and together they did much to
change the climate of opinion. The strength of Sinn Féin in the
beginning was that it did not carry solely the political connotation
that the name would nowadays imply. Indeed, it did not even
assume that name until 1905, six years after its founder, Arthur
Griffith had started the newspaper, *United Irishman*, in which he
developed his ideas. Griffith was born in Dublin in 1871. Trained
as a printer, he spent some time in South Africa, but returned to
edit the new paper. He found in Dublin a multitude of little clubs
—some enthusiastic for the language, some nostalgic for Thomas
Davis, some concerned with economic development and others
with political programmes—and to all of them he gave a voice. At
the outset it seemed an unmistakably republican voice, for in the
first issue of *United Irishman* Griffith proclaimed that he accepted
the nationalism of '98, '48, and '67. Yet, though he might recite
the magic numbers of Irish insurrection, Griffith's feet were firmly
planted on the ground. An armed uprising he, like most people,
took to be out of the question in any foreseeable future and he
bent his efforts to converting a new generation to his doctrine of
self-reliance. He wanted his fellow-countrymen to recover their
identity as a separate people, which meant not only that they must
cherish their language, their literature, and their history, but also
that they must foster their own industries and cease to take both
their goods and their opinions ready-made from England.

Griffith was not alone in his emphasis on the need for self-
reliance. Just as he was launching *United Irishman*, another journalist appeared on the scene. This was D. P. Moran, who in 1900
founded *The Leader*, which he was to own and edit for nearly
forty years. In this paper, week after week, he poured out his scorn
upon the layers of pretence and humbug which, in his view,
stifled nearly every kind of constructvie activity in Ireland. He
was the sworn enemy of cant—or, in the Irish version, which he
made a household word, 'ráiméis'—and he hit out at it violently
wherever he found it. Since he found it nearly everywhere he
made many enemies, but since, like Griffith, he opened his col-
umns to a variety of viewpoints, *The Leader* became one of the

most widely read papers of the time. Moran was both negative and positive. He was not only against cant, he was also against drink, and against the Irish parliamentary party, and against everything that ministered to English influence in Ireland. He was for industrial development, for the Irish language and Irish culture, for Catholicism, for independence provided it was not some sham political settlement. In some ways an extremely bigoted person, he invented a whole series of rude names for people or groups he did not like—the liquor interest was 'Mr. Bung', Protestants were 'sourfaces', Catholics who aped English ways were 'shoneens', Griffith and his friends (with whose political ideas Moran disagreed) were 'the Green Hungarian Band', and so on *ad nauseam*.

But Moran was capable of much more than mere vilification. Between 1898 and 1900 he had begun to develop the ideas to which, when they appeared in book form in 1905, he gave the generic title, *The Philosophy of Irish Ireland*. In this seminal book, a key statement of the case against the dominant culture, he started from the bleak proposition that the Irish were so far gone in servility to their conquerors as to be almost beyond redemption. The recent celebrations of the centenary of the 1798 rising, with their ineffectual harking back to Wolfe Tone, struck him as an obscene mockery. 'What was it all'. he asked, 'but a mere parade of men being dragged further and further after the British chariot, or rather . . . going open-eyed that way, the while they cried out to deceive themselves and the world: 'We are not English!' If not, what are they? let me ask again. They have discarded their language and they know nothing of their literature. The prevailing manners at the present time are the resultant of good nature, the influence of Lover's novels, and a half-hearted attempt to copy the English lower-middle class, who, in the shape of cheap holiday trippers, are a dream of gentility to the Irish snob. Sulky West Britons is the only name by which the great majority of "nationalists" can be designated.'[1]

Moran was not impressed by the efforts hitherto made to retrieve the situation, and with impartial venom he attacked cultural and political myths alike. Particularly he detested the

[1] D. P. Moran, *The Philosophy of Irish Ireland* (Dublin, 1905), p. 9.

movement to create an Irish literature in the English language. The 'Celtic note', as he contemptuously called it, seemed to him 'one of the most glaring frauds that the credulous Irish people ever swallowed'.[2] As for the 'Protestant nation' and Grattan's famous constitution of 1782, which Griffith was just then holding up as a model, that, too, was a fraud. 'It did not mark a noble but a disastrous epoch and turning point in Irish history. It sent us adrift in a new world by which we were first corrupted and then eaten up; it set up a new temple before which . . . we have made the greatest sacrifice in our power—the sacrifice of our national character.'[3]

Yet, if 1782 was the year when, as Moran put it, 'the country became fixed, not as an Irish nation, but as an English province', his reaction to all who had subsequently tried to put this right was comprehensively dismissive. They had a wrong order of priorities, he insisted. Thinking always of political independence, they had never stopped to define the nation whose independence they sought. Moran himself had no doubts about the matter. 'The foundation of Ireland is the Gael, and the Gael must be the element which absorbs.' Viewed from this standpoint, O'Connell had been a disaster. Indeed, just because he was a giant in his own way, he was a gigantic disaster. 'He did more than any other man . . . to kill the Gaelic language and distinctive nature of the people.' As for Young Ireland, despite Davis's noble aim of reconciliation, they only compounded O'Connell's folly. 'The worst thing they did . . . was that they brought into life a mongrel thing, which they called Irish literature, in the English language.'[4]

Much of this was no more than the frustration of a man sensitive to atmosphere and stifled by the false values, as he saw it, that he found all about him. But Moran was, according to his lights, constructive also. He had two lights to steer by—industrial development and the language revival. Only by determined pursuit of these objectives could true national unity be achieved. Effectively, this meant that the Gaelic League must bear the brunt of the struggle. But the League, he stressed, could not simply be

[2] Ibid., p. 22. [3] Ibid., p. 34. [4] Ibid., pp. 37, 43.

left to preach to a largely anglicized population in a language that population could no longer understand. For many years to come there would have to be 'an active, vigilant and merciless propaganda' in English.

It was this propaganda that Moran set himself to provide in *The Leader*, a propaganda for the Gaelic culture in what he described as 'the battle of two civilisations'.[5] Because he believed with all his force that this was precisely what it was he regarded the popular identification of politics with nationality as a hopeless delusion. 'Unless we are a nation', he declared, 'we are nothing, and the growth of a civilisation springing from the roots of one of the oldest in Europe will alone make us a nation, give us scope to grow naturally, give us something to inspire what is best in us, cultivate our national pride and self-respect, and encourage our self-dependence.'[6]

This message, constantly reiterated, made Moran one of the most formidable opponents of cultural fusion. He was formidable because he refused to admit that a middle ground was possible. Any emanation of what he regarded as English culture, whether it was *Tit-Bits* or the poetry of W. B. Yeats, was suspect because, being in the tongue of the foreigner, it was a threat to the survival, and revival, of Irish. For him, the battle of two civilizations was the cultural form of the age-old struggle between England and Ireland. In that struggle each individual had to choose which side he or she would be on. Most people, no doubt, were indifferent to, or simply unaware of, Moran's imperatives, but no artist of that generation could ignore them. And though they disagreed on nearly everything under the sun, Moran would certainly have accepted Yeats's definition of the dilemma facing all Irish writers,

---

[5] 'The Battle of Two Civilisations' was the title of the last of Moran's essays in *The Philosophy of Irish Ireland*, though the essay was originally published in *New Ireland Review* in August 1900. Yeats used an almost identical phrase in a public lecture in 1903. 'If you examine to the root a contest between two peoples, two nations, you will always find that it is really a war between two civilisations, two ideals of life' (cited by Robert O'Driscoll, 'Return to the Hearthstone', in Andrew Carpenter (ed.), *Place, Personality and the Irish Writer* (Gerrard's Cross, 1977), p. 49).

[6] D. P. Moran, *The Philosophy of Irish Ireland*, p. 114.

'to choose whether they will write as the upper classes have done, not to express but to exploit this country; or join the intellectual movement which has raised the cry that was heard in Russia in the 'seventies, the cry "to the people" '.[7]

It was in the theatre that this dilemma was posed most acutely and specifically, partly because nearly all the leading figures of the renaissance converged upon it, but still more because it was the most public, and therefore the most publicized, of the arts available to innovators at that time. At first the omens seemed good. In 1900, as we saw earlier, Hyde's Irish play, *The Twisting of the Rope*, had received its first performance, and that same year the Irish Literary Theatre was transformed into the Irish National Theatre Society which, instead of employing English professional actors, used instead the little group of amateurs who gathered round the brothers William and Frank Fay. The first offerings of the 'national theatre' were immediately successful. One was AE's version of *Deirdre* and the other was Yeats's play, *Cathleen ni Houlihan*, which made such a powerful appeal to the patriotic emotions of its audience that in after years its author came to regard it as a stage on the road to 1916 and to ask himself 'Did that play of mine send out/Certain men the English shot?'[8]

So far, then, só good. By 1902 the theatre seemed well established and in harmony with the Irish revival. But what few people had yet perceived was that the directors of the theatre had a purpose which might or might not coincide with the purpose of those who wished to restore a native Irish culture, but which was independent of, indeed largely indifferent to, the Gaelic movement. In selecting their plays, as Lady Gregory and Yeats repeatedly made clear, they were concerned to choose only what seemed to them to be good, and to go on giving those 'good' plays until the public accepted them. By 'good' they, especially Yeats, intended an aesthetic judgement. 'This movement', he wrote, 'should be important even to those who are not especially interested in the Theatre, for it may be a morning cockcrow to that impartial meditation about character and destiny we call the

[7] W. B. Yeats, *Explorations*, p. 83 (*Samhain*, 1901).

[8] W. B. Yeats, 'The Man and the Echo', *Collected Poems* (London, 1950), p. 393.

artistic life in a country where everybody, if we leave out the peasant who has his folk-songs and his music, has thought the arts useless unless they have helped some kind of political action, and has, therefore, lacked the pure joy that only comes out of things that have never been indentured to any cause.'[9] It was, in effect, a movement partly of reaction against the commercial theatre, though partly also of emphasis upon the primacy of art over propaganda. But it was no less an aristocratic movement, since Yeats and Lady Gregory, in imposing their aesthetic doctrines equally upon their actors and their audiences, were behaving as to the ascendancy manner born. The assumption that *they* knew what was best, that *they* should dictate the form of the theatre and the selection of its plays, made sound artistic sense, perhaps—the Abbey Theatre could hardly have been born otherwise—but the price that had to be paid for this lordly independence was an increasing vulnerability to criticism should their ideal and the Irish Ireland ideal ever seriously diverge.

Such a divergence would probably have occurred sooner or later, but it was precipitated by the work of John Millington Synge. Synge was a product of the Protestant middle class and a graduate of Trinity College. An introverted, silent, stubborn man, he loved the Irish countryside, hating towns and all conventional social life. His ambition was to write and, as the (possibly apocryphal) story has often been told, the direction of his life was changed when Yeats, meeting him in Paris in 1896, gave him the famous advice to go to the Aran islands and discover a world that had not yet been celebrated in literature.[10] There, and also in Wicklow, Synge found both the themes and the language (a

---

[9] W. B. Yeats, *Explorations*, p. 103 (*Samhain*, 1903).

[10] This may in fact have been a piece of Yeatsian hindsight. Synge had his own reasons for going to Aran in 1898, some eighteen months after Yeats's 'advice'. These included a family connection (an uncle, the Reverend Alexander Synge, had been incumbent there in 1851) and a growing fascination with Celtic culture stimulated by the work of the Breton writer, Anatol Le Braz, and by attending the lectures of d'Arbois de Jubainville at the Sorbonne. Besides, Synge had already studied Irish in Trinity, so that Aran, pre-eminently an Irish-speaking area, was an obvious place for him to go. The evidence for this revision of an oft-told tale is in Mark Mortimer, 'Yeats and Synge: an Inappropriate Myth', *Studies*, vol. lxvi (winter, 1977), 292–8.

highly stylized English, using Irish speech-forms and rhythms) which absorbed him until he died in 1909 just before his thirty-eighth birthday. His importance to the theatre was that he combined lyrical beauty and comic invention with a firmly unsentimental view of life as it was lived among the peasants. Little interested in aesthetic discussion, he was quite unyielding where his own work was concerned. What he had seen he had seen, what he had written he had written, and that was all. He had, as Yeats remarked, 'that kind of intense, narrow personality which necessarily raises the whole issue'.[11]

The issue Synge was to raise was raised most starkly by the famous riots that greeted the first production of *The Playboy of the Western World* in 1907, but four years earlier another of his plays, *In the Shadow of the Glen*, had provoked a violent controversy which bore no less directly on the battle of the two civilizations. When Synge arrived upon the scene the issue had indeed already been defined and his function was so to sharpen it that it could no longer be ignored or blurred by bland generalizations. In reality, there was not one issue, but several. The first was whether there could or should be an Irish literature in English. A second was whether, through poetry and drama and the other arts, it was still possible to fashion a cultural identity for Ireland separate from that of England, in which Irishmen of different traditions could feel themselves at home. And finally, there was the issue of whether or not the artist should be free to write what he pleased without the compulsion of having to subordinate his work to a cause, however elevated that cause might be.

With so many large questions to be answered it is not surprising that the replies should have been varied and confused. We may, however, distinguish three main responses—the cosmopolitan, the Anglo-Irish, and that of Irish Ireland. The archetypal cosmopolitan was Edward Dowden, the Professor of English at Trinity College. Dowden was a Shakespearean scholar, the biographer of Shelley, an early admirer of Walt Whitman, and one of the few Irish critics to recognize the importance of Ibsen. His

[11] W. B. Yeats to John Quinn, 15 Feb. 1905 (Allan Wade (ed.), *The Letters of W. B. Yeats* (London, 1954), pp. 447–8).

interest in modern literature was unquestioned and his friend,
John Eglinton, was not exaggerating greatly when he said that for
many years Dowden's mind was 'probably the first point touched
by anything new in the world of ideas outside Ireland'.[12] But
Dowden always closed that mind against the possibility of creating
a recognizably Irish literature. 'The direction of such work as I
have done in literature', he said, 'has been (to give it a grand name)
imperial or cosmopolitan, and though I think a literature ought
to be rooted in the soil, I don't think a conscious effort to promote
a provincial spirit tends in that direction.'[13] James Joyce, who once,
perhaps on the basis of their shared Ibsenism, vainly solicited
Dowden's help for a job in the National Library, expressed the
same idea more concretely, and crudely, in his youthful essay,
'The Day of the Rabblement'. Having first supported the Irish
Literary Theatre, he turned savagely against it when it put on
Hyde's *Twisting of the Rope* and the Yeats-Moore version of the
story of Diarmuid and Grania. By thus surrendering to 'Irishness',
Joyce believed that Yeats and his friends had compromised with
the multitude and their theatre 'must now be considered the
property of the rabblement of the most belated race in Europe'.[14]
Joyce, it is true, did not altogether lose touch with the leaders of
the new movement, but henceforth his ironic and ambitious gaze
was increasingly fixed on the continent.

Yet it was neither of these, but John Eglinton, a friend of
Dowden's and in due course also a specimen under Joyce's micro-
scope, who emerged as the most articulate exponent of cosmopolitanism. His prime target was the Irish Ireland ideal of a Gaelic
literature expressing and strengthening the sense of nationality.
If art were thus to be regarded as the handmaid of patriotism,
Eglinton argued, the results would be deeply divisive. 'Sooner or
later,' he wrote, 'Ireland will have to make up its mind that it is
no longer the old Gaelic nation of the 5th or 12th, or even of the
18th century, but one which has been in the making ever since

[12] E. A. Boyd, *Appreciations and Depreciations* (Dublin, 1918), p. 152.
[13] Ibid., p. 157.
[14] James Joyce, 'The Day of the Rabblement', in E. Mason and R. Ellmann
(ed.), *The Critical Writings of James Joyce* (London, 1959), pp. 70, 71–2.

these islands were drawn into the community of nations by the Normans.'[15] This, naturally, was vehemently contested by the Irish Ireland school. 'We are working', wrote one of them, 'for a new Irish civilisation, quite distinct from the English' and that could only be achieved by developing an autonomous Irish language and literature. Without it, 'we may be but cultural slaves and *seonini*'.[16]

Eglinton was unimpressed. He opposed the isolating influences both of Gaelicism and of the nationalistic writings of Thomas Davis. The one, by insisting upon the primacy of a language nobody else knew, was bound to cut Ireland off from the main stream of European culture. And the other, which was offered as a temporary substitute, was almost worse, because Davis had given 'a sort of religious or idealistic status to modern Irish patriotism which it has retained'. To demand that 'Irishness' should be the touchstone of whatever new literature was to be written, was to condemn the Irishman to speak in his national rather than in his human capacity. This, he insisted, was a kind of death:

Literature must be free as the elements; if that is to be cosmopolitan, it must be cosmopolitan . . . and I should like to see the day of what might be called . . . the de-Davisization of Irish national literature, that is to say, the getting rid of the notion that in Ireland a writer is to think first and foremost of interpreting the nationality of his country, and not simply of the burden he is to deliver.[17]

It was symptomatic of the gulf opening between the two camps that just as Eglinton was attacking the Davis tradition for having subordinated art to nationalism, others attacked it for not having been nationalistic enough. When a journalist, W. P. Ryan, wrote a book complaining that the Young Irelanders did not really fit into the Irish Ireland canon, D. P. Moran was quick to explain their fundamental error. 'Their country was Anglo-Ireland but they called it in perfect good faith Ireland.'[18]

That Anglo-Ireland was not Ireland was a lesson the quintessential Anglo-Irishman, John Synge, had now to learn. His play,

[15] John Eglinton, 'The Island of Saints', in *United Irishman*, 8 Feb. 1902.
[16] W. P. Ryan in *United Irishman*, 22 Feb. 1902.
[17] *United Irishman*, 31 Mar. 1902.
[18] *The Leader*, 11 Jan. 1902.

In the Shadow of the Glen, dealt with a theme familiar enough in the Irish countryside, the loveless marriage of a young woman to an old man. Synge's Nora, like Ibsen's Nora, solved her problem by turning her back on it, eloping with a tramp to face the uncertainties of an existence which, however hard, was better than the living death to which the conventional pieties would condemn her.

At once the nationalist critics were roused to fury. Arthur Griffith condemned the play as a lie, based upon an old Greek tale, *The Widow of Ephesus*, which Synge was trying to pass off as Irish, whereas 'all of us know that Irish women are the most virtuous in the world'. 'Men and women in Ireland marry lacking love', he conceded, 'and live mostly in a dull level of amity. Sometimes the woman lives in bitterness—sometimes she dies of a broken heart—but she does not go away with the tramp.'[19]

The reaction here is significant—it is an instinctive recoil from anything that does not square with the idealized national stereotype. But still more significant was the way in which Griffith and others widened the controversy to include the larger issue of the relationship between art and nationality. Yeats, taking up the cudgels for Synge, was nevertheless in a difficulty. He still regarded himself as a nationalist, but he had never constrained his art to the needs of his nationalism and said so now. A true nationalist, he argued, was one 'who is prepared to give up a great deal that he may preserve to his country whatever part of her possessions he is best fitted to guard'.[20] Griffith had no difficulty in disposing of such equivocation, opening the way as it seemed to do towards the dreaded cosmopolitan heresy. 'Cosmopolitanism', he replied, 'never produced a great artist nor a good man yet and never will.' 'If [the National Theatre] substitutes *Cathleen ni Houlihan* by *The Widow of Ephesus*, we are certain it will pass and leave not a wrack behind. When it ceases to be national, it will also cease to be artistic, for nationality is the breath of art.'[21]

A week later Yeats riposted with one of his most pugnacious pieces, 'The Irish National Theatre and Three Sorts of Ignorance'.

[19] *United Irishman*, 10 and 17 Oct. 1903.
[20] *United Irishman*, 17 Oct. 1903.
[21] *United Irishman*, 17 Oct. 1903.

In this he identified first 'the more ignorant sort of Gaelic obscurantist, who would have nothing said or thought that is not in
country Gaelic'; next, 'the more ignorant kind of priest who,
forgetful of the great traditions of his church, would deny all
ideas that might perplex a parish of farmers . . . of half-educated
artisans'; and finally, 'the politician, and not always of the more
ignorant sort, who would reject every idea which is not of immediate service to his cause'. Could they not discard these kinds
of ignorance and serve Ireland 'without giving up the search for
truth, the respect for every kind of knowledge'?[22] But Griffith
was implacable. Conceding that Yeats was a sincere nationalist,
he suggested that what was chiefly wrong with him was that he
was not a wise one. And he laid his finger on a fatal flaw in the
poet's position. 'Mr Yeats does not give any reason why if the
Irish National Theatre has now no propaganda save that of good
art it should continue to call itself either Irish or National. If the
Theatre be solely an Art Theatre then its plays can only be fairly
criticized from the standpoint of art. But whilst it calls itself Irish
National its productions must be considered and criticised as Irish
National productions.'[23]

This was, in its way, unanswerable. Yeats's counter definition
of national literature as 'the work of writers who are moulded by
influences that are moulding their country, and who write out of
so deep a life that they are accepted there in the end', did not even
satisfy its author and certainly would not have satisfied Griffith.[24]
The immediate outcome was that both Maud Gonne and Douglas
Hyde withdrew from the Irish National Theatre Society, so that
Yeats found himself drifting further away both from militant
nationalism and from pacifist Gaelicism. He always believed that
this quarrel prepared the way for the much greater storm that
broke over the production of *The Playboy of the Western World* in
1907. By then the Abbey Theatre was in being, and, although it
was far from conforming to Yeats's ideal, he, and Lady Gregory
and Synge, were as determined as ever that their sole criteria in

[22] *United Irishman*, 24 Oct. 1903.
[23] *United Irishman*, 24 Oct. 1903.
[24] W. B. Yeats, *Explorations*, p. 156 (*Samhain*, 1904).

deciding what plays to perform should be artistic, not nationalistic.

In the *Playboy*, the central character, Christy Mahon, becomes a village hero when he boasts of having murdered his father. But after the battered, but very much alive, father arrives to claim him, Christy's popularity dramatically declines. This story, also, Synge maintained he had found in the west of Ireland, but his critics would have none of it. They were outraged almost equally by a play which openly referred to women in their shifts, and which made a hero, or pseudo-hero, out of a parricide. These two kinds of prudery, the sexual and the moral, raised once more the cry that the theatre was intent upon defiling the good name of Ireland. Bernard Shaw, writing a few years later when the *Playboy* was under attack in America from the Fenians of the Clan-na-Gael, caricatured the arguments inimitably. 'The Clan-na-Gael . . . suddenly struck out the brilliant idea that to satirise the follies of humanity is to insult the Irish nation, because the Irish nation is, in fact, the human race, and has no follies, and stands there pure and beautiful and saintly to be eternally oppressed by England and collected for by the Clan.'[25]

The sequel is well known. When the play opened it was virtually howled down in the third act and rioting continued for a week. The nationalist press condemned it utterly. To the *Freeman's Journal* it was 'an unmitigated, protracted libel upon Irish peasant men and, worse still, upon Irish peasant girlhood'. The *Evening Mail*, more grandly, thought it was perhaps an allegory and that Christy symbolized a nation-killer idolized by Irish men and women. 'If it is an allegory it is too obscure for me. I can not stalk this alligator on the banks of the Liffey . . . If a man is stupid enough to suggest that the Irish people are cannibals or gorillas, my hand will not fumble for the sword-hilt.'[26]

It fell to Yeats to mount the counter-attack. After the first storm was over, he took the stage himself to defend the play in open debate, almost provoking another riot in the process. Part

---

[25] Lady Gregory, *Our Irish Theatre* (Coole Park edn., Gerrard's Cross, 1972), chap. 6.

[26] Cited in D. H. Greene and E. M. Stephens, *J. M. Synge, 1871–1909* (New York, paperback edn., 1961), p. 242.

of his defence was simply a declaration of aristocratic independence. Others might withdraw plays because of intimidation, the Abbey directors would not. 'We have not such pliant bones, and did not learn in the houses that bred us a so suppliant knee.' But behind this arrogance was something more fundamental. What Yeats was really challenging was the narrowness of the new, puritanical nationalism, allied as this was (or so he believed) with a growing tendency towards mob rule:

Some seven or eight years ago [he said] the National movement was democratised and passed from the hands of a few leaders into those of large numbers of young men organised into clubs and societies. These young men made the mistake of the newly enfranchised everywhere; they fought for causes worthy in themselves with the unworthy instruments of tyranny and violence. Comic songs of a certain kind were to be driven from the stage, everyone was to wear Irish cloth, everyone was to learn Irish, everyone was to hold certain opinions, and these ends were sought by personal attacks, by virulent caricature and violent derision.[27]

Even to keep the *Playboy* in production was, he claimed, a victory. 'Gentlemen of the little clubs and societies,' he said, 'do not mistake the meaning of our victory; it means something for us, but more for you.' What it meant, he suggested—too optimistically, as it turned out—was that the youth of the country were becoming weary of this tyranny. 'They wish again for individual sincerity, the eternal quest of truth, all that has been given up for so long that all might crouch upon the one roost and quack or cry in the one flock.'[28] A little later, he developed this theme further when defending the decision to take the *Playboy* to London:

Ireland is passing through a crisis in the life of the mind greater than any she has known since the rise of the Young Ireland party, and based upon a principle which sets many in opposition to the habits of thought and feeling come down from that party . . . Many are beginning to recognise the right of the individual mind to see the world in its own way, to cherish the thoughts which separate men from one another . . . instead of those thoughts that had made one man like another if they could, and have but succeeded in setting up hysteria and insincerity in place of confidence and self-possession. To the Young Irelanders, who have still the ear of Ireland, though not its distracted mind, truth was

[27] W. B. Yeats, *Plays and Controversies* (London, 1923), pp. 194-5.
[28] Ibid., p. 196.

historical and external and not a self-consistent personal vision, and it is but according to ancient custom that the new truth should force its way amid riot and great anger.[29]

Yeats seems here to be desperately trying to hold a middle position between the anonymity of cosmopolitanism and the parochialism of Irish Ireland. He still had not abandoned the hope of a fusion between the Anglo-Irish and the Gaelic cultures, out of which would come a literature written in English that would be of European stature, yet unmistakably Irish in its style and content. But his grand vision was based upon a misreading of contemporary reality. Soon he was to learn more about the nature of that reality and the searing experience would cause him to recoil into the poetry of disenchantment. Indeed, with John O'Leary dead and Synge soon to die, the theory of aristocratic leadership he had been formulating under Lady Gregory's tutelage was already beginning to take shape. For a brief moment in the early years of the new century it almost seemed as if this theory might have some basis in fact. After a generation of land war and land legislation the tide had turned towards the break-up of the large estates and the creation of a multiplicity of small, independent farmers. To complete the process the landlords needed a larger financial incentive to sell, and this was provided in 1902 by a land conference summoned by Lady Gregory's nephew, Captain John Shawe-Taylor, on his own initiative. The terms there agreed by the landlords' and tenants' representatives prepared the way for the Wyndham Act of 1903 and though this needed subsequent amendment, it is rightly regarded as marking the moment when the grip of the ascendancy on the land was at last decisively loosened. The immediate effect of this social revolution was to confirm the gentlemen of Ireland in their congenital schizophrenia. On the one hand, it made excellent sense to sell while the going was good, retaining often no more than a demesne farm in the neighbourhood of the 'Big House'. On the other hand, the Wyndham Act was unmistakably the culminating stroke in the steady separation of the landed class from the source of their traditional authority. Not surprisingly, it

[29] Ibid., pp. 197–8.

left them confused and vulnerable, conscious only that they could no longer rely upon the British connection to protect them.

Yet we must not over-emphasize their insecurity. Recent scholarship suggests that just as there were fewer bad landlords than nationalist propaganda asserted, so the relationship between landlord and tenant was far more complex, far more intimate, than easy generalizations about the inevitability of a class war would lead one to suppose.[30] The relaxed and deferential society depicted in the lighter works of Somerville and Ross, or in the novels of George Birmingham, did still exist. So also, of course, did the seeds of decay, as Somerville and Ross brilliantly perceived in *The Real Charlotte*, but the decay was gradual and for most landlords life in the first decade of the new century was a strange chiaroscuro. The dark shadow of ultimate expropriation indeed hung over them, but it could be relegated to the borders of consciousness because upon 'real life'—fox-hunting, shooting, fishing, lawn-tennis, house-parties, the Viceregal season—the sun continued to shine as if nothing had changed or was ever likely to change.

This tendency to go on living in the past naturally affected the attitude of the Protestant ascendancy as a whole towards any movement seeking to create a new Ireland based upon the fusion of cultures. Most of them had no difficulty in deciding against it, so far as they were aware of it at all. Their reaction was likely to be much the same whether they thought the country was going to the dogs, or whether they thought things had never been better. If the outlook was stormy, then there was no option but to stand one's ground and hold what one had. If the outlook was settled, then why not let life go on in its usual agreeable fashion?

Holding such views, it was understandable that the gentry, even those who had profited from the Wyndham Act, should look askance at any attempt to extend the conference idea to wider fields of nationalist-unionist co-operation. Such an attempt was actually made in 1903 by Shawe-Taylor, and by the chairman of

[30] See, for example, Barbara Solow, *The Land Question and the Irish Economy, 1870–1903* (Cambridge, Mass., 1971), *passim*, and T. R. Henn, *Last Essays*, pp. 207–20.

the land conference, Lord Dunraven, this time to settle the university question. The proposal fell flat, but the following year Lord Dunraven and a small group of like-minded landlords created the Irish Reform Association with no less an object than to dispose of the Home Rule issue by substituting a scheme of devolution which would give Ireland an extended system of local government. As a working proposition the scheme was naïve and inadequate, but even so it aroused such fury amongst unionists that the Chief Secretary, George Wyndham, though he repudiated it, was driven from office.

This obscure affair bears upon the conflict of cultures in several important ways. First, the fury of the onslaught indicated the deep anxiety of most unionists about political, as opposed to socio-economic, change. Secondly, it was noticeable that the real venom of the attack came from the Ulster unionists, who immediately formed a body of their own, the Ulster unionist council, which in the coming years was to play a major part in defining and organizing the 'separateness' of their province from the rest of Ireland. Most important of all, the storm over devolution marked the end of the landlord flirtation with constructive unionism. Dunraven and Shawe-Taylor had made their bid to bridge the gulf between their order and the nationalist majority, because they had sensed that the only future for the former governing class would be to participate in the new Ireland from within. Their difficulty was that they could never persuade their fellow-landlords that the change really was coming and that it would be devastating. And so the landed gentry continued on the path towards destruction which Standish O'Grady had marked out for them in 1900. 'Aristocracies come and go like the waves of the sea; and some fall nobly and others ignobly. As I write, this Protestant Anglo-Irish aristocracy which once owned all Ireland from the centre to the sea, is rotting from the land in the most dismal farce-tragedy of all time, without one brave deed, one brave word.'[31]

This was not quite fair, for Sir Horace Plunkett, as we have

[31] Standish O'Grady, 'The Great Enchantment', in *Selected Essays and Passages*, p. 180.

seen, had single-handed done more than any other member of the aristocracy to reconcile two different traditions, two different ways of life. But Plunkett also had fallen on hard times. Always something of the schoolmaster, in 1904 he felt moved to give his pupils, the Irish people, the benefit of his advice by publishing a book, *Ireland in the New Century*. In the course of this he chose to lecture them about their defects of character, most of which he attributed to the politicians and to the Roman Catholic Church. The politicians, he suggested, were so obsessed by the need to destroy English rule in Ireland *before* undertaking major social and economic changes, that they opposed almost automatically any non-political movement as being a diversion from the sole object of their existence. And because they insisted on rigid conformity to their ideology, they stifled individuality, instilled into their followers a dread of public opinion (the basic principle of boycotting, for example), and thus contributed to the shirking of responsibility and the lack of moral courage which Plunkett regarded as two of the more deplorable Irish characteristics.

As for Roman Catholicism, it, also, bore a heavy share of responsibility for this sad state of affairs. Too authoritarian, too apt to induce fatalism in the devout, too ready to divert scant economic resources into unnecessary church-building, its influence, he thought, had been on the whole repressive. It was on the right side on the temperance question, admittedly, and individual priests had done much for their parishes, though the methods they used to inculcate chastity among their flocks contributed to what struck him as the joylessness of Irish country life, which in turn he saw as a major cause of emigration. But with even-handed justice, Plunkett then went on to make the worst of both worlds. Some Protestants, particularly the Ulster Presbyterians, were, he reckoned, mainly to blame for keeping alive a spirit of bigotry, and he deplored especially their addiction to what he called 'the July orgy'. On the other hand, his experience had shown him that the Roman Catholics, while freer from bigotry, 'are apathetic, thriftless and almost non-industrial, and they especially require the exercise of strengthening influences on their moral fibre'. North and south each had virtues the other lacked, but, he con-

cluded comfortably, 'the home of the strictly civic virtues and
efficiencies is Protestant Ireland'.[32] Unfortunately, Protestant
Ireland was slow to recognize Plunkett's own civic virtues and his
undoubted, if tactless, efficiencies. In 1900 he lost his parliamentary
seat to another unionist, and, though he remained at the head of
his Department of Agriculture and Technical Instruction for
another seven years, nationalist pressure after the Liberals came to
power in 1906 brought about his downfall.

The fate of Dunraven and Plunkett vividly illustrates the
dilemma of the Anglo-Irish. To move out of the accustomed
groove, to liberate a spirit of conciliation, seemed impossible for
two opposing reasons. On the one hand, the ascendancy at large
could not be persuaded that change was their only salvation. On
the other hand, those with whom the progressive unionists might
have wished to co-operate were never really convinced that
'progressive unionist' was not a contradiction in terms and so
could not bring themselves to bathe in healing waters sprung from
such a tainted source. The result was that the gap between the
cultures grew wider rather than narrower as the years rolled on.
This was epitomized by a strange episode which, though not itself
of the first importance, yet revealed how vulnerable the protagonists of cultural fusion could be when they had both unionists
and nationalists against them.

It arose out of the offer made in 1913 by another of Lady
Gregory's nephews, Sir Hugh Lane, to present his collection of
modern French painting to the city of Dublin if suitable arrangements could be made for housing it. A new gallery was envisaged
and Sir Edwin Lutyens produced an imaginative design for a
building that would span the Liffey. But the money required to
realize this dream was not forthcoming, largely because certain
rich men declined to make substantial contributions on the ground
that the need for such an extravagance had not been demonstrated. The ensuing controversy revealed such an unpleasant
combination of meanness and philistinism among the opponents
of the scheme that Lane angrily withdrew his offer.[33] Among

---

[32] Sir Horace Plunkett, *Ireland in the New Century* (London, 1904), chap. 4.
[33] As is well known, Lane added a codicil to his will, just before he sailed to his

these rich men were Lord Ardilaun of the Guinness family and William Martin Murphy. The latter, who had taken a prominent part in the deposition of Parnell, owned the *Independent* newspaper which had pursued Synge with rancorous venom and earned Yeats's undying hatred as a result. This hatred found expression in the bitter poetry of *Responsibilities* and in the preface to that volume Yeats explained why. Three controversies in his lifetime had stirred his indignation—the Parnell split, the *Playboy* riots, and the Lane pictures. It was no coincidence, he believed, that behind each of them was Murphy, the traducer equally of Parnell, Synge, and Lane, and as such the embodiment of the Catholic bourgeois nationalism which Yeats had come to recognize as his chief enemy:

These controversies [he wrote]—political, literary and artistic—have shown that neither religion nor politics can of itself create minds with enough receptivity to become wise, or just and generous enough to make a nation . . . Religious Ireland—and the pious Protestants of my childhood were signal examples—thinks of divine things as a round of duties separated from life, and not as an element that may be discovered in all circumstances and emotions; while political Ireland sees the good citizen but as a man who holds to certain opinions and not as a man of good will. Against all this we have but a few educated men and the remnants of an old political culture among the poor. Both were stronger forty years ago, before the rise of our new middle class which showed as its first public event during the nine years of the Parnellite split how base at moments of excitement are minds without culture.[34]

As chance would have it, Murphy was also at the centre of a much bigger dispute which occurred in the latter half of 1913. He was the leader of the Dublin employers who locked out their workers when the latter joined the militant trade union (the Irish Transport and General Workers' Union) established by the fiery

---

death on the *Lusitania*, in which he bequeathed the pictures to Ireland after all. Disputing the validity of the codicil, the British government retained the pictures for many years, until agreement was finally reached that the collection be divided in two, part to hang in Dublin and part in London, and that the two sections be exchanged from time to time. In Dublin the pictures were placed first in a gallery in Harcourt Street and then in Charlemont House, which contains the Municipal Gallery of Modern Art. It is pleasant to be able to record that a short time ago Dublin Corporation voted to change the name to the Hugh Lane Municipal Gallery of Modern Art.

[34] Lady Gregory, *Hugh Lane* (London, 1921), pp. 121-2.

orator, James Larkin, and the more intellectual, but also more formidable, James Connolly. The employers believed they were defending property against syndicalist socialism. The workers were fighting not only against high unemployment and low wages, but also against the appalling living conditions which made the Dublin slums among the worst in Europe. After six months of dour struggle the workers went back largely on the employers' terms and, although Larkin's union was not totally destroyed, the outcome was a severe defeat for organized labour.

While the conflict lasted, the workers had not met merely the full force of entrenched capitalism, but also the indifference, and often the hostility, of a society none of whose cultures seemed to have a place for the urban proletariat. The Church, for example, threw its weight against Larkin's movement when it intervened to prevent the children of starving slum families from being sent to England for temporary care, on the ground that their faith would be endangered. And not only the Church, but nearly every section of 'respectable' Dublin seemed to think more about the threat posed by the eruption than about its causes. The Irish parliamentary party were deeply opposed to a trade union movement which might end by taking the labour vote away from them. Arthur Griffith denounced Larkin almost hysterically, because the higher wages he sought for his members would damage the competitiveness of Irish industry. Dublin Corporation, which numbered some slum landlords among its members, shuddered at this explosion from the lower depths. Nearly all the major newspapers, financed as they mostly were by big business, were loud in their condemnation.

Yet some voices were raised on the other side, most notably those of AE and of Yeats. AE, whose co-operative doctrines had had some influence on Larkin, approached the quarrel both as one who hated the inhumanity of the employers and as a prophet who chastized them for their folly. In a famous 'Open Letter to the Dublin Employers', he linked the fate of the aristocracy of industry with the fate that had already befallen the aristocracy of the land. 'The men whose manhood you have broken will loathe you, and will always be brooding and scheming to strike a fresh blow. The children will be taught to curse you. The infant being moulded in the womb will have breathed into its starved body the vitality of hate. It is not they—it is you who are blind Samsons pulling down the industrial order.'[35]

Yeats's attitude was more complex. On 1 November he published in the *Irish Worker*, James Connolly's paper, an article entitled 'Dublin Fanaticism'. It was an attack equally upon unionists and nationalists for exacerbating a dangerous situation:

I do not complain of Dublin's capacity for fanaticism whether in priest or layman . . . but neither those who directed the police nor the editors of our newspapers can plead fanaticism. They are supposed to watch over our civil liberties and I charge the Dublin nationalist newspapers with deliberately arousing religious passion to break up the organisation of the working man, with appealing to mob law day after day, with publishing the names of working men and their wives for purposes of intimidation. And I charge the unionist press of Dublin and those who directed the police with conniving at this conspiracy.[36]

Here Yeats was clearly reaching out beyond the specific incidents which aroused his wrath. He was genuinely moved by the plight of the workers, no doubt, but he was at least as much moved by hatred of that middle class which he had already fought so often on his own behalf, on behalf of Synge, on behalf of Hugh Lane. That William Martin Murphy should again be the foe was only the crowning provocation. But the actual outcome of the fight mattered less to Yeats than the fact that the labour dispute, following so quickly the ignoble quarrel over the Lane pictures, helped to complete that alienation from the squalid Ireland he saw around him and which was the motive force of much of his poetry at this time:[37]

> What need you, being come to sense
> But fumble in a greasy till
> And add the halfpence to the pence,
> And prayer to shivering prayer, until

[35] *Irish Times*, 7 Oct. 1913.
[36] *Irish Worker*, 1 Nov. 1913.
[37] W. B. Yeats, 'September 1913', *Collected Poems*, p. 120. For a penetrating analysis of Yeats's attitude to the labour dispute, see C. Cruise O'Brien, 'Passion and Cunning: an Essay on the Politics of W. B. Yeats', in A. N. Jeffares and K. G. W. Cross (ed.), *In Excited Reverie* (London, 1965), pp. 228–38.

You have dried the marrow from the bone;
For men were born to pray and save,
Romantic Ireland's dead and gone,
It's with O'Leary in the grave.

This recoil from Dublin and from Ireland had serious consequences for Yeats's subsequent attitude to the fusion of cultures
he had fought so hard to bring about. For even though 1916 was
to reawaken his 'Irishness', and even though in 1922 he returned
home to involve himself deeply in the life of his country, an
element of alienation still remained. Others, as we shall see, began
to fight the same fight once more after 1922 in vastly changed
circumstances. But Yeats never again championed cultural fusion
as he had done until about 1907. He would still be capable of
hurling a masterpiece in the teeth of the mob—as he did with
O'Casey's *The Plough and the Stars* in 1926—but this defiance was
essentially a function of the aristocratic habit of mind into which
by 1913 he had irretrievably settled.

From his standpoint he was surely right. It is unlikely that he, or
Lady Gregory, or Hugh Lane, or John Shawe-Taylor, or Horace
Plunkett, or Lord Dunraven, fully understood what was happening while it was happening. But we can see now that collision
rather than fusion of cultures seemed to be the logic of events. This
was true not only of the developing split between north and south,
or of the larger conflict between Ireland and England, but also of
the clash between Irish Ireland and Anglo-Ireland on the narrow
stage of Dublin. The assumption of Yeats and his friends that
Ireland was as wax in their hands after Parnell's fall was a false
assumption. It was false because it underestimated the religious
element in Irish life and largely ignored the political element. Yet
at the moment when Anglo-Irish Ireland was reaching the peak
of its cultural achievement, religion and politics were both waking
to new life.

It is not always realized how active and ubiquitous the Catholic
Church was in the generation before the First World War and how
much it was being stimulated by forces operating inside and outside its own organization. That generation, in fact, experienced

something like a popular religious revival. Thus, for example, devotion to the Sacred Heart of Jesus, intermittent earlier in the century, was greatly stimulated by the Apostleship of Prayer which was vigorously preached from 1887 onwards by the Jesuit, Father James A. Cullen. The magazine of the movement, *Messenger of the Sacred Heart*, rapidly acquired a large circulation and was used by Father Cullen to promote temperance as well as prayer. Many took the pledge against drink and in 1901 the Pioneer Total Abstinence Association was founded to carry the work still further. Frequently the temperance movement was equated with liberation from English domination. 'With fell design,' said one preacher, 'England suppressed our commerce, our factories, our mines, our industries, and left us only the distillery.'[38] The corollary was deceptively simple. As the watchword had it—'Ireland sober is Ireland free'.

In a different, but no less effective way, the Gaelic League helped to strengthen the marriage between religion and nationalism. Most obviously, of course, it could be utilized as a barrier against the flood of immoral literature in English which was a constant worry of the Catholic hierarchy in the decades before 1914. But the current flowed in both directions. Two priests, Father O'Growney and Father O'Hickey, played a major part in the revival of Irish, and the effective founder of the League, Eoin MacNeill, was in no doubt that true religion and the native language were deeply interfused. 'When we learn to speak Irish,' he observed, 'we soon find that it is what we may call essential Irish to acknowledge God, His presence, and His help, even in our most trivial conversation.'[39]

Naturally, also, with the Catholic revival went an idealization of the peasant, who was cherished equally by the Church and by the League. To this idealization even Douglas Hyde lent a willing hand. 'The Irish Gael is pious by nature', he wrote. 'He sees the hand of God in every place, in every time and in everything . . .'

[38] P. J. O'Farrell, *England's Irish Question* (New York, 1971), p. 225. I am much indebted to Professor O'Farrell's analysis of this and cognate questions in part 3, chap. 7, of his book.
[39] Ibid., p. 229.

The Protestant Hyde was somewhat taken aback, however, to find that what he regarded as the link between Gaelicism and Christianity was regarded by others as a connection between Gaelicism and Catholicism.[40] The obverse of the cult of the peasant was a recoil from corrupt and stinking towns and cities, and from that it was but a step to condemn 'modern civilization' in general, more particularly as exemplified by England.[41] This kind of isolationism could only end by being both narcissistic and insensitive. Thus, on the one hand, Cardinal Logue looked forward in 1914 to a time when Ireland would be not only the most virtuous nation on the earth—'as, indeed, she was at present'—but also the most sober. And in March 1912, with the Ulster question at crisis point, a writer in the *Catholic Bulletin* could see the north as a field ripe for missionary endeavour. 'The day of missionary heroism is at hand, and to be utilised first of all in our own country . . . To bring into the bosom of Holy Church the million of our separated brethren is a most attractive programme, and there is in it enough of the heroic to engage and claim the hearts of Irish Catholics.'[42] That

[40] Ibid., p. 230.

[41] Modern civilization in its English form was not the only enemy. The Church struck with equal vigour at modernism within its own ranks, as three instances from this period will show. One was the fate of the 'modernist' priest, Father Jeremiah O'Donovan, who, after being largely responsible for the beautification of the new cathedral at Loughrea, County Galway, fell foul of the authorities, left the priesthood, and, as Gerald O'Donovan, wrote several interesting autobiographical novels (e.g. *Father Ralph* (1913) and *Waiting* (1904)) now undeservedly forgotten. A second example was the stormy career of the theology professor at Maynooth, Walter McDonald, whose *Reminiscences of a Maynooth Professor* (London, 1925, paperback abridgment, Cork, 1967) show him to have been constantly in trouble with his bishops for his outspoken comments on contemporary issues and on the hierarchy's failure to grapple with them; he was not dismissed, but his writings were frequently censored and refused publication. The third case is that of a layman, the journalist W. P. Ryan, whose would-be progressive newspaper, the *Irish Peasant*, had to leave its base in Navan after Cardinal Logue had condemned it as 'a most pernicious anti-Catholic print'. Ryan continued it in Dublin, changing its name after a time to the *Irish Nation*, but in 1910 had to give up the unequal struggle. His account of the incident is to be found in his novel, *The Plough and the Cross* (1910) and in his study, *The Pope's Green Island* (London, 1912). Both throw much light on the restiveness of the younger Catholic intellectuals in the face of ecclesiastical conservatism. Nevertheless, the authority of the Church remained substantially intact.

[42] P. J. O'Farrell, *England's Irish Question*, p. 245.

northern Protestants might have a different view of their destiny seems never to have entered the writer's head.

The marriage between Catholicism and Gaelicism was fatal to the hopes of the Protestant Anglo-Irish protagonists of cultural fusion. Catholicism and Gaelicism, and the nationalism they nourished, were reacting primarily against England. It was English manners and morals, English influences, English Protestantism, English rule, that they sought to eradicate. That was the main battle. Compared with it, the battle between Irish Ireland and Anglo-Irish Ireland was ultimately of secondary importance. Yeats and his friends were casualties in that battle, no doubt partly because what they said and wrote would in any event have offended the susceptibilities of Gaelic and Catholic nationalism. But in a deeper sense they were incidental casualties, the walking wounded of a war in which the enemy was always England.

Another way of putting this is to say that politics was reasserting its normal role in Irish life. The long-drawn-out Parnellite split had indeed turned the minds of the new generation in different directions, but those directions could never lead far outside the political context while Ireland remained under English rule. Every cultural initiative, every artistic experiment, every work of literature, was liable to be judged by a single criterion—whether it helped or hindered the breaking of the English connection. Therefore, the Catholic and the Gaelic revivals were just as much political as was the rise of Sinn Féin. The journalism of *The Leader* and the campaign for Irish industry were equally political, because they were bent upon developing an Irish resistance to all things English. As for those Anglo-Irish writers who claimed to have no propaganda but that of good art, and who wanted to look beyond England and Ireland to Europe, they were doomed almost before they had begun. They had believed that a basis for reconciliation existed, whereas none did exist, at least on terms which they would have regarded as acceptable. As Protestants for the most part, as products of the still distrusted ascendancy, they could have been welcomed into the new nationalism only if, like Parnell, they had turned their backs completely on the tradition that had bred them. This they instinctively refused to do. To deliver up their integrity to the rule of the majority was a sacrifice they could not contemplate. Still less could they contemplate it when they saw what the majority had done to Parnell. It is no accident that in Yeats's poems of alienation of this period that tragic figure reappears as a symbol of rejection.

Given the uneven balance of forces, it was remarkable that the Anglo-Irish champions of cultural fusion should have achieved as much as they did. Simply to have survived without having been dominated by what Joyce called 'La Bestia Trionfante' was no mean feat. Yet it is significant that Joyce, bred up as he was in the atmosphere of Irish Ireland, never quite believed that the Anglo-Irish could maintain their momentum and still continue un-hampered to live and work in the country. He himself, knowing the strength of the undertow, resorted to silence, exile, and cunning. And while in an artistic sense he never really left his native city, his insight into the Irish paralysis, of which Dublin was the centre, denied him any hope of changing the fundamentals of the situation. He would fly by those nets of nationality, language, and religion. The Anglo-Irish, born to rule and confident that they could control events, thought otherwise. Much of the cultural history of Ireland in the twentieth century was to be the history of their disenchantment.

Yet there was a double irony implicit here. For if it was true that politics were reasserting its traditional role, it was also true that the chief work of the generation between the death of Parnell and the Easter Rising had been to lay bare as never before the socio-cultural roots of difference in Irish society. Of those roots and that difference all political solutions in future would have to take account. But if it was true, too, that everything in Ireland seemed to be fated to be subordinated to the struggle against England, then the further irony was that after England's political grip had been loosened, her cultural influence in large measure persisted. How both these ironies affected Irish attitudes both to the diverse cultures within the island, and to the dominant culture pressing upon it from outside, will be the principal themes of my remaining lectures.

4

The Revolutionary Generation

'THERE has been nothing more terrible in Irish history than the failure of the last generation.' Thus Patrick Pearse in 1915, opening his pamphlet, *Ghosts*, with an onslaught upon the constitutional nationalists who had occupied the centre of the political stage since the death of Parnell. How, he asked himself, had these men sinned, that they should have come to such impotence? 'Is it that they are punished with loss of manhood because in their youth they committed a crime against manhood? . . . Does the ghost of Parnell haunt them to their damnation?'[1]

Pearse did not stay for an answer to his own rhetorical question because he knew the answer already. He was sure that the real reason for the failure of the previous generation lay deeper. 'They have conceived of nationality as a material thing, whereas it is a spiritual thing . . . They have not recognised in their people the image and likeness of God. Hence the nation is not to them all holy, a thing inviolate and inviolable, a thing that a man dare not sell or dishonour on pain of eternal perdition.'[2] With this indictment Pearse reminds us that the battle between the civilizations had entered a new phase. To understand that phase we have to understand also the passions which moved him and those who, with him, made the Easter Rising, for those passions were to have a long and influential history that is not yet ended.

The Rising was the work of many diverse individuals and it can be viewed at many different levels. From the political standpoint its authors regarded themselves as being in the direct

[1] Patrick Pearse, *Political Writings* (Dublin, n.d.), pp. 223–4.
[2] Ibid., pp. 224–5.

line of descent from Wolfe Tone and as the modern exponents of the revolutionary, conspiratorial republicanism last demonstrated by the Fenians in their abortive rebellion of 1867. One of the most fanatical organizers of the 1916 insurrection, Thomas Clarke, provided a direct link with the Fenian tradition in his own person, embodying as he did in all its crude but potent simplicity the driving force of that tradition—an unrelenting hatred of England and an absolute conviction that the English connection could only be broken by an armed uprising to establish an independent Irish republic.

Yet, although this was the *raison d'être* of the Irish Republican Brotherhood which claimed the ultimate responsibility for the Rising that began on Easter Monday, 1916, the genesis of that event was far more complex than Tom Clarke knew, or cared to know. To call the Rising a 'revolution of the intellectuals' would not wholly explain that complexity, but thinkers and poets nevertheless did play a central role, both in formulating its programme and in setting it in motion. No fewer than four of the seven signatories of the Proclamation were writers and together they gave to this climactic moment an ideological content which reflected some of the most important cultural preoccupations of Ireland in the years preceding their insurrection. They were not a homogeneous group. Three of them, indeed, may be thought of as having a common view, but the fourth, James Connolly, represented a different tradition and had a different vision.

The three who thought broadly alike were Patrick Pearse, Thomas MacDonagh, and Joseph Plunkett. What they had in common was that all were young, all were poets, all were Gaelic enthusiasts, all were romantic revolutionists, all were Catholics with a strong inclination towards religious, or quasi-religious, mysticism. The chief of them was Pearse, who was born in Dublin in 1879, the son of an English monumental sculptor long settled in the city. Introduced to Irish at the age of eleven or twelve, Pearse became one of its foremost advocates, both as editor of the leading journal of the Gaelic League and as the founder and inspirer of the bilingual school, St. Enda's, where he exerted a powerful influence upon a whole generation of pupils.

In the launching of this school he was helped by Thomas Mac-Donagh, also born in 1879, a graduate of University College, Dublin, and a lecturer in English at that college. MacDonagh had for a time acted as tutor to Joseph Plunkett, who was eight years his junior, and who afterwards collaborated with him in theatre work and in producing an Irish Ireland periodical, the *Irish Review*.

Of the three, Pearse was not only the best known but also the most explicit in shaping and defining the new nationalism. Recently, and no doubt in reaction against half a century of uncritical adulation, there has been a tendency in some quarters to diminish Pearse as a revolutionary force, but when the pendulum of historical assessment eventually comes to rest, it is hard to believe that he will not continue to occupy a place of central importance in the evolution of the Irish Ireland movement, looking back as he did towards the idealistic beginnings of that movement and forward towards what it might become in action. For the understanding of both the early and the mature Pearse his mysticism is the essential key. This was evident as early as 1897, in an address written and delivered before his eighteenth birthday. 'The Gael', he declared, 'is not like other men, the spade and the loom and the sword are not for him. But a destiny more glorious than that of Rome, more glorious than that of Britain, awaits him: to become the saviour of idealism in modern intellectual and social life . . .'[3] As his thought developed, however, it found room for the sword, if not for the spade or the loom. In his educational experiment at St. Enda's he laid great stress upon heroic legend as an inspiration for the young; this led him straight to the Irish sagas and in particular to the story of Cuchulainn, the Ulster hero who had died fighting against the invader. Over the entrance to St. Enda's there was a fresco round which was emblazoned the words attributed to Cuchulainn in the Ulster cycle, 'I care not though I were to live but one day and one night if only my fame and my deeds live after me.' Yet, as a devout

---

[3] Cited by D. Thornley, 'Patrick Pearse—the Evolution of a Republican', in F. X. Martin (ed.), *Leaders and Men of the Easter Rising: Dublin 1916* (London, 1967), pp. 155–6.

Catholic, Pearse could not look purely to pagan inspiration and it was significant that in an attack on the anglicization of Irish education in his pamphlet, *The Murder Machine*, he linked the legendary figure of the warrior, Cuchulainn, with the real figure of the missionary saint, Colmcille.

For Pearse they were as one, because they both exemplified the devotion that could inspire one man to suffer, and perhaps die, for his people. 'The old Irish system,' he wrote, 'pagan and Christian, possessed in pre-eminent degree the thing most needful in education: an adequate inspiration. Colmcille suggested what that inspiration was when he said, "If I die it will be from the excess of love that I bear the Gael". A love and a service so excessive as to annihilate all thought of self, a recognition that one must give all, must be willing to make the ultimate sacrifice—this is the inspiration alike of the story of Cuchulainn and of the story of Colmcille, the inspiration that made the one a hero and the other a saint.'[4] In this, it is clear, his thought was already being touched by the Messianic strain which had appeared and re-appeared in Irish writing repeatedly since the death of Parnell.[5] And in November 1913 he gave this theme a much more precise formulation when, speaking at the annual commemoration of Wolfe Tone, he seemed to forecast not only another insurrection, but that it might end as Tone's had done. 'Such,' said Pearse, 'is the high and solitary destiny of the heroes: to turn their backs to the pleasant paths and their faces to the hard paths, to blind their eyes to the fair things of life . . . and to follow the far, faint call that leads them into battle or to the harder death at the foot of a gibbet.'[6]

Messianism necessarily involved a religious view of history and as the prospect of action drew nearer both Pearse and his two friends gave their nationalism an increasingly religious quality, more strictly a quality of Catholic mysticism, from which in their poetry they freely reproduced themes, images, signs, and

    [4] Patrick Pearse, *Political Writings*, p. 25.
    [5] F. S. L. Lyons, 'The Parnell Theme in Literature', in Andrew Carpenter (ed.), *Place, Personality and the Irish Writer* (Gerrard's Cross, 1977), pp. 69–95.
    [6] Patrick Pearse, *Political Writings*, pp. 58–9.

symbols. Joseph Plunkett probably went further down this road than the others. He is known to have been much influenced by St John of the Cross and by the works of Johann Tauler, and some of the sayings of St John in particular appear almost unchanged in his poetry.[7]

For Plunkett and MacDonagh, as indeed for Yeats also in his very different circumstances, one of the most evocative symbols was the rose, which had many significations. It was, for example, the flower of the Rosicrucians, a symbol of Christ, and also a symbol of the Irish nation. Thus Plunkett, in 'The Little Black Rose Shall Be Red At Last', addressing himself as a lover to the dark rose, the traditional image of conquered Ireland, could end with this couplet:

> Praise God if this my blood fulfils the doom
> When you, dark rose, shall redden into bloom.[8]

And Thomas MacDonagh brought these two themes of mysticism and nationalism even closer together in two verses of his poem 'Barbara':

> When the life of the cities of Europe goes
> The way of Memphis and Babylon,
> In Ireland still the mystic rose
> Will shine as it of old has shone.
>
> O rose of Grace! O rare wild flower,
> Whose seeds are sent on the wings of Light!
> O secret rose, our doom, our dower,
> Black with the passion of our night.[9]

What comes through here is not merely the renunciation of the world that we would expect from the poets' bias towards mysticism, but also a clear indication that both Plunkett and MacDonagh were already imbued with the doctrine of the blood-sacrifice. It was Pearse, however, who gave this doctrine its most

[7] For this reference I am indebted to Richard J. Loftus, *Nationalism in Modern Anglo-Irish Poetry* (Madison and Milwaukee, 1964), p. 139.

[8] Joseph Plunkett, *Poems* (Dublin, 1916), pp. 59–60.

[9] Thomas MacDonagh, *Poetical Works: Lyrical Poems* (Dublin, 1916), p. 138.

direct and powerful expression. In November 1913 he publicly renounced the Gaelic League, as he had known it. It had only been a stage in the education of those who wanted to serve Ireland, he said, and it had become a spent force. It had been a prophet, but it was not the Messiah. 'I do not know if the Messiah has yet come, and I am not sure that there will be any visible and personal Messiah in this redemption: the people itself will perhaps be its own Messiah, the people labouring, scourged, crowned with thorns, agonising and dying, to rise again immortal and impassible.'[10]

The Gaelic League, he was now saying, had brought into Ireland 'not peace but a sword'.[11] Nationhood could not be achieved other than by arms. 'We may make mistakes in the beginning and shoot the wrong people; but bloodshed is a cleansing and a satisfying thing, and the nation which regards it as the final horror has lost its manhood. There are many things more horrible than bloodshed; and slavery is one of them.'[12] A man capable of using this language before the world war had broken out was certain to become still more obsessed by bloodshed after the fighting had begun. But, since this dire obsession has often been credited to him alone, it is proper to point out that it was shared by others, both in Ireland and in the wider world beyond. It is not, perhaps, so surprising to find that militant socialist, James Connolly, endorsing Pearse's view that Ireland had become so degraded that only 'the red tide of war on Irish soil will ever enable the Irish race to recover its self-respect', but it is rather more startling to find him echoing Pearse's sacrificial language. 'Without the slightest trace of irreverence', Connolly wrote in February 1916, 'but in all due humility and awe, we recognise that of us, as of mankind before Calvary, it may truly be said "without the shedding of blood there is no redemption".'[13] But Pearse and Connolly had already been anticipated, indeed outvied, by a popular and revered novelist, Canon Sheehan, renowned in

[10] Patrick Pearse, *Political Writings* ('The Coming Revolution'), p. 91.

[11] Ibid., p. 96.

[12] Ibid., pp. 98–9.

[13] C. D. Greaves, *The Life and Times of James Connolly* (London, 1961), pp. 318–19.

Ireland (if not outside it) for his ability to combine nationalism and religion in his work. In one of his books, *The Graves at Kilmorna*, written in 1912–13, his characters use such phrases as these: 'The country is sinking into the sleep of death; and nothing can awake it but the crack of the rifle . . . We may also have to teach from our graves! . . . the political degradation of the people which we have preached with our gaping wounds will shame the nation into at least a paroxysm of patriotism again! . . . it is the fools that do all the world's great work. Then the world calls them heroes.' And again, '. . . as the blood of martyrs was the seed of saints, so the blood of the patriot will be the sacred seed from which alone can spring new forces, and fresh life, into a nation that is drifting into the putrescence of decay'.[14]

Canon Sheehan was an unlikely, and no doubt an unconscious, agent of the *Zeitgeist*, but he was swimming with a current that was running strongly through the western civilization of his day. In literature after literature we find a preoccupation with the themes of carnage and bloodshed, of conspiracy and subterranean explosion, of 'the breaking of nations'. These anticipations of global conflict, becoming more numerous and more specific in their detail from about 1870 onwards, have been admirably charted by I. F. Clarke in his *Voices Prophesying War*, and they give substance to George Steiner's comment that by about 1900 'there was a terrible readiness, indeed a thirst, for what Yeats was to call "the blood-dimmed tide" '.[15] Pearse may or may not have been aware of the European tendency—though he was well-read in literatures other than his own and, within his own, could hardly have overlooked Canon Sheehan—but whatever fires burned beneath the surface of his mind before 1914, they erupted almost uncontrollably once the war had begun. Increasingly, metaphors of violence and of sacrifice recur in the speeches and writings of the last two years of his life. Both themes were explicit, for example, in his oration at the graveside of the old Fenian, O'Donovan Rossa, in August 1915. 'Life springs from death,' he

---

[14] Cited in P. J. O'Farrell, *Ireland's English Question*, pp. 231–2.
[15] I. F. Clarke, *Voices Prophesying War, 1763–1884* (Oxford, 1966), *passim*; George Steiner, *In Bluebeard's Castle* (London, paperback edn., 1971), p. 27.

proclaimed, 'and from the graves of patriot men and women spring living nations.'[16] And he followed this a few months later by an exultant hymn to war which, more perhaps than anything else he wrote, conveys the *hysterica passio* that lay at the root of his personality. 'The last six months have been the most glorious in the history of Europe . . . It is good for the world that such things should be done. The old heart of the earth needed to be warmed with the red wine of the battlefields. Such august homage was never offered to God as this, the homage of millions of lives given gladly for love of country.' War might be terrible, he said, but it was not evil; it was the things that made war necessary which were evil. And when war came to Ireland, she must welcome it as she would welcome the angel of God. 'We must not flinch when we are passing through that uproar; we must not faint at the sight of blood. Winning through it, we (or those of us who survive) shall come into great joy. We and our fathers have known the Pax Britannica. To our sons we must bequeath the Peace of the Gael.'[17]

It is still disputed amongst historians as to whether the few hundred men who went out on Easter Monday, 1916, to wage war against the superior power of the British Empire did so in the expectation of victory or in the foreknowledge of defeat. The rank and file, perhaps, may have hoped for some miraculous deliverance in the form of German aid, but the leaders, knowing how vain that hope had become in the days immediately preceding the Rising, can have had no such comfortable illusion. The poets, especially, assumed that they would die in battle, or perhaps on the scaffold, for they shared a common myth. They had deliberately chosen, as has been well said, 'to image themselves as sacrificial heroes taken from the old mythologies of torn gods'.[18] The recurrent theme of the blood-sacrifice in their poetry can have no other explanation. And for Pearse, as always the most explicit of them, that one man, or a few men, should die for the

[16] Patrick Pearse, *Political Writings*, pp. 136–7.

[17] Ibid., pp. 216–18.

[18] W. I. Thompson, *The Imagination of an Insurrection: Dublin, Easter 1916* (New York, 1967), p. 139.

people was an imitation of Christ in the most literal sense possible. In after years one of his sisters recalled that her brother's greatest devotion was to Calvary, 'to Christ crucified and to the crucifix', and this seems to confirm the fusion in his own mind of the legend of Cuchulainn and the life of Christ.[19] With their renunciations, the fabled and the real, of the ordinary goals and pleasures of life he identified himself totally and in one of his late poems—in fact called 'Renunciation'—he disowns the senses one by one until only death confronts him:

> I have turned my face
> To this road before me
> To the deed that I see
> And the death I shall die.[20]

And, in an almost uncanny anticipation of the execution of his brother and himself, in another late poem he imagines his mother accepting with pious resignation the departure of her two sons.

> To break themselves and die, they and a few,
> In bloody protest for a glorious thing.[21]

It comes as no surprise, therefore, that two of the poets, MacDonagh and Pearse, should have written plays on the theme of the hero seeking single-handedly to confront the enemy. Pearse's hero, MacDara, characteristically invokes the crucifixion as his model. 'One man can free a people as one Man redeemed the world . . . I will stand up before the Gall [the foreigner] as Christ hung naked before men on the tree.'[22] Was this blasphemy? In another poem, 'The Fool', he shrugged off the accusation, deriding the 'wise men' who condemned the fool for having dared to dream his dream:

> O wise men, riddle me this: what if the dream come true?
> What if the dream come true? and if millions unborn shall
> dwell

[19] Mary Pearse, *The Home Life of Padraig Pearse* (Dublin and Belfast, 1934), p. 141; R. J. Loftus, *Nationalism in Modern Anglo-Irish Poetry*, pp. 159–60.
[20] Patrick Pearse, *Plays, Stories, Poems* (Dublin, 1924), pp. 324–5.
[21] Ibid., p. 333.
[22] Ibid., p. 44.

In the house that I shaped in my heart, the noble house of
   my thoughts?[23]

We can, see then, that the poets of the Rising shared a common
view of the destiny that awaited them. Not only that, they shared
a common cultural standpoint which looked forward, as Pearse
once defined it, to an Ireland 'not free merely but Gaelic as well;
not Gaelic merely, but free as well'.[24] By thus carrying to the
extreme of logic the doctrines alike of Gaelicism and of republicanism, and by doing this within the framework of their Catholic
mysticism, they transformed the battle of the two civilizations.
Whereas, up to 1916, that battle had been fought in the world of
literature and journalism and the theatre, where both sides were
fairly evenly matched, the Easter Rising, with its emphasis upon
national redemption through the shedding of blood, was to
change the balance dramatically. But it was to change more than
the balance between Anglo-Irish Ireland and Irish Ireland. For
within the ideology which underlay the Rising there was a
socialist as well as a nationalist strand, and not the least remarkable
aspect of the way in which Pearse imposed his view upon the
movement is that he and his fellow-poets were able to persuade
James Connolly to march and die with them.

It does not seem that the romantic revolutionaries, as a group,
paid much attention to social conditions and needs, though
Pearse was something of an exception. He was, he said in October
1913, when the Dublin labour troubles were at their height,
'nothing so new-fangled as a socialist or a syndicalist'. 'I am old-
fashioned enough to be both a Catholic and a nationalist.'[25] As a
compassionate man, he sympathized with the plight of the workers
and had even a good word to say for James Larkin, but it was
only near the end of his life that he began to try to envisage in
concrete terms what kind of society might lie on the other side of
that revolution he craved. In the last of his major pamphlets, *The
Sovereign People*, he took the position that national sovereignty
must be exercised for the good of *all* the men and women who

[23] Ibid., pp. 335–6.
[24] Patrick Pearse, *Political Writings*, p. 135.
[25] Ibid., pp. 176–7.

made up the nation. Indeed, he even went so far as to accept that 'no private right to property is good as against the public right of the nation'. Realizing, perhaps, that he was teetering on the brink of socialism, he hastened to add that there was nothing divine or sacrosanct in whatever specific arrangements might be made for the control by the state of the material resources of the nation, but he insisted nevertheless that all property (and he did not disallow private property) should be held subject to 'the national sanction'.[26] This, though vague enough, was inserted into the Proclamation of Independence which he read to the indifferent bystanders outside the General Post Office on Easter Monday. 'We declare the right of the people of Ireland to the ownership of Ireland and to the unfettered control of Irish destinies, to be sovereign and indefeasible.' And again: 'The republic guarantees religious and civil liberty, equal rights and equal opportunities to all its citizens, and declares its resolve to pursue the happiness and prosperity of the whole nation and of all its parts, cherishing all the children of the nation equally, and oblivious of the differences carefully fostered by an alien government, which have divided a minority from a majority in the past.'

This, it is true, does not rise above the level of pious generalization, and it is so innocuous as to raise an important question—how did James Connolly come to sign such a platitudinous document; for that matter, how did he come to be in the General Post Office at all? The question is directly relevant to the clash of cultures in Ireland because, during the decade before the Rising, the two labour leaders, Larkin and Connolly, had presented to Irishmen an alternative ideology to the prevailing Catholic, Gaelic nationalism, which, had it achieved what they desired, might have had a direct effect upon the balance of forces inside Irish society, and especially on the relations between north and south. But although both men were at bottom religious, and found no ultimately irreconcilable conflict between their doctrines and Catholicism, their commitment to socialism so alarmed the guardians of traditional morality that their efforts to realize in Ireland the syndicalist ideal of the 'one big union' which would

[26] Ibid., pp. 337–40.

eventually overthrow the existing order, if necessary through the weapon of a general strike, had brought upon them accusations of communism and of anti-Christian bias.

I suggested in an earlier lecture that Larkin had aroused the hostility of the Catholic bishops and clergy by his extremism. But their objections went far deeper than a recoil from the methods he used against the employers in 1913. It has been plausibly argued that one reason why the resurgence of militant republicanism between 1914 and 1926 took the Church so much by surprise—as it clearly did—was that the defenders of religion were preoccupied by what seemed to them a far more terrible and imminent peril—the rising tide of socialism. Grotesquely exaggerated as this fear must in retrospect appear to be, it has to be set against the background of the labour war of 1913 and of the seething discontent in the Dublin slums. To churchmen, Larkin and Connolly were guilty on a double count. In the first place, the creed they preached was rank materialism. As the *Catholic Bulletin* put it: 'A full stomach was put before the people as the one thing in life worth striving for . . . the worst passions of our nature, and these alone, were appealed to; pride, cupidity and selfishness . . . The upright Irishman for the time disappeared, and all of the brute that was in him was drawn out and fed.' But secondly, and worse, this socialism was seen as an *English* phenomenon, yet one more facet of the threat to Irish purity from the proximity of the pagan island:

For the past twenty years the Gael has been crying . . . for help to beat back the Anglicisation he saw dragging its slimy length along—the immoral literature, the smutty postcards, the lewd plays and the suggestive songs were bad, yet they were merely puffs from the foul breath of a paganised society. The full sewerage from the *cloaca maxima* of Anglicisation is now discharged upon us. The black devil of Socialism, hoof and horns, is amongst us.[27]

With Larkin's departure to America in 1914 the more flamboyant apostle of socialism was removed, but there remained James Connolly. He was a much more formidable opponent, not only because he was of far higher intellectual calibre, but because

[27] *Catholic Bulletin*, Nov. 1913, cited in P. J. O'Farrell, *Ireland's English Question*, pp. 269–70.

he directed his efforts deliberately towards removing sectarian divisions from the labour movement. He had not got far with this before 1916—indeed the violence of the Ulster resistance to Home Rule (resistance in which workers too participated) indicated the almost impossible odds against which he had to struggle. Yet, in his calm insistence, at the end of a famous controversy with the Jesuit Father Kane in 1910, that socialism transcended religious differences, Connolly was striking a note which, had he lived, might have had many reverberations. For him the enemy was capitalism, first, last, and all the time. It must go, he wrote: 'And in the work of abolishing it, the Catholic and the Protestant, the Catholic and the Jew, the Catholic and the Freethinker, the Catholic and the Buddhist, the Catholic and the Mahommetan will co-operate together, knowing no rivalry but the rivalry of endeavour towards an end beneficial to all.'[28]

To advocate unity among the workers was one thing, to throw in his lot with the rebellion of a tiny minority of nationalists was quite another, even if some of them, notably Pearse, were more sympathetic to his standpoint than many contemporaries realized. Connolly was well aware that his participation in the Rising would disconcert at least some of his comrades. 'They [the socialists] will never understand why I am here', he told his daughter just before his execution. 'They will all forget I am an Irishman.'[29] He seems in fact to have done what he did in the belief that in the circumstances of the time, and with European socialism in disarray, a political act might yet be made the prelude to the socio-economic revolution towards which his life's work had been directed.[30] It was, admittedly, a forlorn hope, as he himself realized. 'We are going out to be slaughtered,' he told a friend on Easter Monday, and when the friend asked if there was no chance of success Connolly replied, 'None whatever'.[31]

[28] O. Dudley Edwards and B. Ransom (ed.), *James Connolly: Selected Political Writings* (London, 1973), p. 126.

[29] C. D. Greaves, *The Life and Times of James Connolly*, p. 338.

[30] O. Dudley Edwards, *The Mind of an Activist: James Connolly* (Dublin, 1971), pp. 65–83.

[31] W. O'Brien (ed.), *Labour and Easter Week: a Selection from the Writings of James Connolly* (Dublin, 1966 printing), p. 21.

The sequel bore him out. With his death before a firing-squad, and with Larkin's continued absence in America, the labour movement came to be ruled by trade unionists concerned primarily to improve the conditions of their members within the existing framework of society. True, when an Irish parliament, the first Dáil, met in January 1919, it heard and accepted a Democratic Programme which was in some respects close to the social radicalism of Pearse's *The Sovereign People*. But not only had this Programme been considerably toned down before its presentation to the Dáil, no one pressed seriously for its implementation, which would in any event have been virtually impossible in the years of Anglo-Irish war and civil war that lay ahead. Connolly's dreamed-of revolution therefore became what one historian has called it—'the social revolution that never was'.[32]

The elimination of what might, without too great abuse of language, be called ecumenical socialism meant that the Gaelic nationalism epitomized by the Rising was left face to face with its old enemy—the English power in Ireland. That power was if anything strengthened in the early years of the war. Although it would be wrong to say that the war was ever popular—except, perhaps, in the north-east where it afforded an opportunity for Ulster loyalism to express itself in action—there was in the initial stages a relatively high level of recruitment. By April 1916 there were 150,000 Irishmen on active service, of whom two-thirds had joined the forces since the outbreak of war. If we extend the description 'Irishmen' to those of the second and third generation living in England or in the dominions, the total who fought in the Great War was just short of half a million, of whom 50,000 died.[33] Among them were many who were as dedicated nationalists in the parliamentary tradition as the men of 1916 were in the republican tradition; by fighting on the allied side they believed themselves to be fighting for the rights of small nations and they hoped that out of the inferno Ireland would emerge as one of

---

[32] Patrick Lynch, 'The Social Revolution that Never Was', in T. Desmond Williams (ed.), *The Irish Struggle, 1916–1926* (London, 1966), pp. 41–54.

[33] Henry Harris, 'The Other Half Million', in O. Dudley Edwards and F. Pyle (ed.), *1916: the Easter Rising* (London, 1968), pp. 101–15.

those small nations whose right to self-government might be recognized.

But if the English connection seemed thus to be strengthened by a shared idealism, there were other more material considerations. The war offered not just service in the trenches but also employment in the factories. It was an insatiable consumer of Irish labour and of Irish produce and for the farmers, in particular, the economics of the Union had never seemed so favourable. This was, however, much less true of the towns and cities. The cessation of some kinds of demand, and the diversion of production away from ordinary consumer goods, created much unemployment, and this grew worse as time went on. Concentration on the war effort meant that the extensive rebuilding which was so badly needed in Dublin and Belfast and other places was indefinitely postponed, so that the slums, with all their familiar evils of overcrowding, disease, and high mortality, continued to fester. Indeed, since the price of essential foodstuffs rose steeply, the condition of the poor actually deteriorated. Worst of all, from 1915 onwards, the threat of conscription hung over the country. Between 1916 and the spring of 1918, resistance to this threat became increasingly vocal and determined, and although the government at the last moment recoiled from the large-scale use of force which would have been needed to apply compulsory military service, no single factor operated more effectively than this one to inflame anti-English sentiment over most of Ireland.

The growing discontent was, of course, greatly intensified by the mishandling of the aftermath of the Rising and by the many ineptitudes of government policy in the succeeding two years. As is well known, the immediate popular reaction in Dublin to the insurrection was one of bitter recrimination against the men who had brought ruin to the city in vainglorious pursuit of an obviously lost cause. But this attitude, as is equally well known, began to be changed by the secret and long-drawn-out executions of the leaders, followed shortly by the trial and hanging of Sir Roger Casement. Possibly even more influential in reversing the current of public opinion was the official assumption that the Rising was the work of Sinn Féin (precisely what it had *not* been), from which followed the fateful decision to arrest and intern in England and Wales large numbers of persons deemed to be Sinn Féiners or sympathizers with Sinn Féin. The prison camps in which these people were held became veritable universities for the new nationalism, and, although most of the inmates were released by Christmas, they were already so indoctrinated that on their return many of them at once became involved in the creation of a much more effective resistance movement than that available to the men of 1916.

Side by side with this development went two others, each significant in a different way. The first was the evident fact that within a few weeks of the executions the dead leaders were being elevated to the status of martyrs. Commemorative masses in the churches were marked by the gathering of large and sullen crowds, threatening some new explosion of violence. Pearse, in particular, was singled out for this kind of idolatry and prayers were already being addressed to him not long after his death. The other significant development was that while this cult of extreme nationalism was growing, the guardians of the constitutional tradition, the Irish parliamentary party, failed disastrously to secure a Home Rule settlement in the wake of the Rising; thereafter they progressively lost the confidence of many even of their previous supporters and were eliminated from Irish politics in the general election of 1918.

The consequence was that in the two years after the Rising the militant nationalism which Pearse had embodied became harder and firmer. Increasing stress was laid upon the separate identity of Ireland and the key to this identity was more and more to be found in its Gaelic and Catholic character. We saw in an earlier lecture that most of those who rose to the leadership of the republican movement came to that movement through the Gaelic League. In 1915 the Gaelic League itself formally abandoned its non-political stance, and the links between republicanism and Gaelicism were further strengthened when, after the executions, the leadership of both Sinn Féin and the Irish Volunteers was combined in the person of de Valera, whose commitment to the language was absolute.

The Catholic character of the new nationalism did not depend solely upon the semi-religious cults which grew up around the names of the dead leaders. Far more important was the fact that in 1916, for the first time in the modern history of Ireland, the sympathy of the hierarchy was enlisted on behalf of men who had taken up arms to overthrow the civil power. True, in the early days of the war the bishops had spoken out on the allied side, taking the standard Home Rule line that Ireland's cause was best served in the trenches. True, also, they did not encourage or sanction the Rising. But after it was over their attitude changed in much the same way as that of the laymen changed and for much the same reasons. The tone was set by Bishop Edward O'Dwyer of Limerick, long regarded as a 'Castle bishop', sympathetic to the existing regime. Declaring publicly that the executions were an outrage, he went on to condemn the military rule that followed the collapse of the Rising as 'one of the worst and blackest chapters in the history of the misgovernment of this country'.[34] Perhaps he would not wholly have agreed with the words a nun used to him in June 1916, but the sentiment she expressed was one which many churchmen came rapidly to share. 'It is very pleasant to see how the hearts of the people are turning towards the poor fellows who fell in Dublin. Their deaths have touched a chord of religion and nationality that were hardly ever more beautifully united.'[35] The rebellion, as O'Dwyer himself observed, had been hopeless, but not fruitless. 'It has galvanised the dead bones in Ireland and breathed into them the spirit with which England has had to reckon.' As for the broader position of Catholicism, it was well summed up by the Rector of the Irish College at Rome in a St Patrick's Day sermon in 1918. 'Wrong is not less a wrong because it is decreed by a legislature; and illegal resistance or evasion became the natural protection against immoral laws. And so the Catholics of Ireland rightly disowned what force made them endure.'[36]

This hardening of Catholic and nationalist opinion in the south

[34] P. J. O'Farrell, *Ireland's English Question*, p. 284.
[35] Ibid., p. 268.
[36] Ibid., p. 287.

left the Protestants there, the southern unionists as they were often called at this time, in dangerous isolation. The war itself had already weakened their position. There were few county families which did not have sons on active service and many of these families suffered heavy losses. They were harassed by succession problems, by rising taxation, by the inexorable pressure of the land laws which left them little more than their home-farms and demesne lands. Yet they clung obstinately to what they had, and the young Cork novelist, Brinsley MacNamara, expressed the mood of the rising generation when he looked wonderingly at those whom he called 'the old, old men', drawn back as by some mysterious magnet to their decayed mansions and impoverished estates. 'They had done a thing that was against nature,' he reflected, 'by making themselves aliens in two countries. If only they had seen in the beginning that it was quite impossible for them ever to become Englishmen . . . By God, they might have given Ireland their culture and their courage! It was their pride! The accursed pride of the land had blinded them.'[37]

That this verdict should have missed the mark so comprehensively was an ominous foretaste of the ability of the new Ireland to forget important parts of its past. Not only did the writer seem unaware that to give their culture to Ireland was precisely what some of the Anglo-Irish had tried to do, and not wholly in vain, before 1914, but his basic assumption, that they could never become Englishmen, overlooked the fact that they had never tried to become Englishmen. As we have seen, they had always thought of themselves as Irishmen, though it was also true that simply to be Irish had never been enough for them. They had seen Ireland always in the context of the Empire which so many of them served. The essence of their tragedy was that that Empire was now about to repudiate them at the very moment when they had spent their blood so prodigally on its behalf.[38]

[37] Brinsley MacNamara, 'Irishmen of today: III, the old, old men', in *Irish Statesman*, 6 Sept. 1919.

[38] In these revolutionary years a few individuals among the Anglo-Irish did indeed turn their backs upon their own caste and, like Parnell before them, seek to identify themselves wholly with the nationalism of their day. Erskine Childers, Robert Barton, Maud Gonne, Constance Markiewicz, Roger Casement, Alice

The succession of events between 1916 and 1922 cruelly exposed their vulnerability. Three things in particular contributed to this. The first was the obvious fact that, committed as they were to the war, they could never regard the Rising as other than a stab in the back, a betrayal of those other Irishmen who, only a few weeks later, fell in their thousands on the Somme. Not surprisingly, they were unsparing in their condemnation of the insurrection. Their principal newspaper, the *Irish Times*, clamoured for the ruthless extirpation of treason. 'The surgeon's knife has been put to the corruption in the body of Ireland, and its course must not be stayed until the whole malignant growth has been removed ... Sedition must be rooted out of Ireland once for all ...'[39] And, not to be outdone, the Protestant Archbishop of Dublin, Dr J. H. Bernard, wrote to the London *Times*, supporting the imposition of martial law. 'This is not the time for amnesties and pardons, it is the time for punishment, swift and stern.'[40]

Dr Bernard's *alma mater*, Trinity College, was even more directly concerned with the suppression of the Rising. Its Provost was now the same Mahaffy who had derided the Irish language a generation earlier, and who, more recently, in November 1914 had forbidden 'a man called Pearse' to speak in the College lest he might make an anti-recruiting speech; with a son serving in France, it was not difficult to predict the line Mahaffy would take. But in any event circumstances reinforced inclination. The College, lying astride the insurgents' communications, occupied a key strategic position. Guarded at the outset by its own Officers' Training Corps, it was quickly occupied by the army and on its

---

Stopford Green, and Darrell Figgis are among the leading examples. Fate was not kind to them on the whole. One or two—Barton and Mrs Green—having made limited and specific contributions, moved quietly into the wings of history. Maud Gonne and Constance Markiewicz, though secure in the hearts of the Dublin poor, paid a heavy price for their deracination in personal happiness and even in personal beauty, as Yeats repeatedly pointed out. Casement, as we have seen, was hanged, Figgis committed suicide, and Childers, having taken the republican side in the civil war, was captured and shot on the orders of the Free State government which contained some of his former closest associates.

[39] *Irish Times*, 1 May 1916.
[40] *The Times*, 5 May 1916.

ancient cobblestones were parked the eighteen-pounder guns which helped to drive Pearse and his men from their head-quarters. Inevitably, this physical identification of the College with the military arm, though in the strictest sense involuntary, helped to reinforce the idea which gained ground increasingly in succeeding decades, that Trinity was 'anti-national' and still the bastion of an exclusive Anglo-Irish culture, even though in December 1921 the Board of the College passed a resolution supporting the settlement which established the Irish Free State as a self-governing dominion, and expressing the wish that in the building of the new Ireland 'Trinity men should take an active and sympathetic part'.[41]

The hostility of the southern unionists towards the Rising was only one of three factors contributing to their isolation. The other two were closely connected and both were products of the deteriorating political situation between 1916 and 1922. The first was the total inability of the British government to prevent the revival of militant republicanism, which in turn precipitated the Anglo-Irish war of 1919–21 and the Irish civil war of 1922–3. The second was the failure to devise any form of Home Rule which would contain the Protestant north-east within an all-Ireland state ruled by an Irish government responsible to an Irish parliament. The formal partition of the island in 1920–1 thus ensured that the Anglo-Irish in the twenty-six counties would be a tiny and impotent minority where before they had been part of a large and powerful minority. But worse still were the circum-stances in which the new state of Northern Ireland came into being. Between 1920 and 1922 there was constant friction between the Irish Republican Army and the forces of the Crown which in 1922 nearly led to open war between the two parts of Ireland. Protestants in Belfast and elsewhere responded by fierce attacks on the Catholic population in their midst and they in turn reacted to the establishment of the new state by virtually boycott-ing it. These events largely determined subsequent patterns of

[41] F. S. L. Lyons, 'The Minority Problem in the Twenty-Six Counties', in Francis MacManus (ed.), *The Years of the Great Test, 1926–39* (Cork, 1967), pp. 97–8.

behaviour. Northern Protestants were confirmed in their hatred and fear of southern republicanism. Northern Catholics were locked into a position of non-co-operation and political inferiority. In both communities the already entrenched siege mentality was still further intensified.

For the Protestants in the south the anarchy of these years had dire consequences. The Anglo-Irish war began with a series of attacks upon the police, to which force the Anglo-Irish had contributed most of the officers. Now they, as well as their men, came under fire and some died. Nor were they alone. The gentry in their country residences were easy targets. Soon they began to be visited by armed bands, at first in search of weapons, then, during the civil war, to 'discourage' them from giving allegiance to the newly established Irish Free State. The threat, indeed the actuality, of assassination became almost commonplace, as did the destruction of great or ancient houses. Since these included, among many others, Lady Gregory's ancestral home in Galway (Roxborough), George Moore's house in Mayo, and Sir Horace Plunkett's house, Kilteragh, near Dublin, it seemed by the end of 1923 as if the Anglo-Irish tradition was destined to end in fire and ruin.

Yet in reality this was not so. While some families tore up their roots, to leave Ireland for ever, many remained and some still play their accustomed role in a greatly changed countryside.[42] Moreover, although most of the Anglo-Irish were content to let the storm roll over them and lie low until the tolerant promises of the new regime could be tested in performance, this was not true of all. On the contrary, an indomitable minority of the minority set themselves to fight again the battle of the two civilizations in

---

[42] One of those who not only stayed but evolved from extreme unionism to what has been called 'non-partisan Irishism' was the eccentric but extraordinarily open-minded landlord, Colonel George O'Callaghan-Westropp, who achieved notoriety, if not fame, as the organizer of the Irish Farmers' Union formed in the confused years after 1916 to protect the interests of landowners and 'small' farmers alike. He was a larger than life representative of an Anglo-Irish type still too little noticed by historians—the man or woman in whom love of place transcended divisions based on origins, religion, or politics. His personality and career are brilliantly described in David Fitzpatrick, *Politics and Irish Life, 1913–1921* (London and Dublin, 1977), especially chaps. 2 and 7.

the vastly more unpromising circumstances of the Anglo-Irish war and its aftermath. It is a measure of the tenacity of that tiny band, but even more perhaps of the diminished strength of the culture they represented, that with few exceptions they were the same people who had fought the same battle in the years before 1914.

In the new phase of the debate three men were to be of paramount importance—Yeats, AE, and Sir Horace Plunkett. Of these three, Yeats was not to make his main impact until after he came back to live permanently in Ireland, and even then, as we shall see, his standpoint was markedly different from what it had been before 1914. When the Rising broke out he had been staying with William Rothenstein in Gloucestershire. His host later recalled the gravity with which Yeats received the news, but had also the impression that he was somewhat piqued that he had not been consulted about what appeared to be a poets' revolution.[43] Like nearly everyone else, Yeats was taken by surprise and thrown completely off balance. A letter to Lady Gregory conveyed his confusion: 'I am trying to write a poem on the men executed—"terrible beauty has been born again". I had no idea that any public event could so deeply move me and I am very despondent about the future. At the moment I feel that all the work of years has been overturned, all the freeing of Irish literature and criticism from politics.'[44] The time was soon to come when this initial foreboding would be amply fulfilled, but in the immediate aftermath of the Rising he felt a powerful impulse to identify himself again with his native country. Within a month he had decided to go back there to live. Within three months he had written his poem (it was, of course, 'Easter, 1916', though it was not published until four years later) and by 1917 he had bought his tower at Ballylee to serve as a summer residence, that tower which was to be so powerful a symbol in the next phase of his poetry. All the same, it was not until 1922 that he took the plunge to return home and involve himself deeply in Irish life.

This delay meant that whatever initiatives could be taken

[43] Stephen Gwynn (ed.), *Scattering Branches* (London, 1940), pp. 46-7.
[44] Allan Wade (ed.), *The Letters of W. B. Yeats* (London, 1954), p. 613.

would be taken by others, in effect by AE and by Sir Horace Plunkett. AE had been, if anything, even more affected by the Rising than Yeats. Like Yeats, he knew many of the leaders, but, unlike Yeats, could see for himself the passions which that event had unchained in Ireland. More than ever he saw the one hope for the future in a reconciliation and not a conflict of traditions. This led him to set much store by the Irish Convention of 1917, through which Lloyd George hoped to persuade representatives of different shades of Irish opinion to agree upon a scheme of self-government for Ireland. AE proposed Sir Horace Plunkett for the chairmanship of the Convention and together they tried hard to make it work. Their hopes were wrecked, however, by the refusal of Sinn Féin to participate and by the intransigence of the more extreme Ulster unionists. By the end of 1917 it was already clear that the Convention was a failure and AE was driven back upon the pen as the one means left to him of insisting upon the need for unity and of reminding his fellow-countrymen that no single culture could claim a monopoly of Irishness. This was the theme of his answer to Yeats's 'Easter, 1916', the poem which he published in the *Irish Times* in December 1917 and which, entitled 'To the Memory of Some I Knew who are Dead and who Loved Ireland', was the only major utterance of that time to mourn the death both of those who fell in the Rising, and those who fell on the western front. Two stanzas, one paying tribute to Thomas MacDonagh and the other to T. M. Kettle, the economist, writer, and nationalist M.P., who was killed on the western front, illustrate how AE, though lacking Yeats's gifts of diction and imagery, could yet achieve his own kind of eloquence:

> I listened to high talk from you,
> Thomas MacDonagh, and it seemed
> The words were idle, but they grew
> To nobleness by death redeemed.
> Life cannot utter words more great
> Than life may meet by sacrifice,
> High words were equalled by high fate,
> You paid the price: You paid the price.

You who have fought on fields afar,
That other Ireland did you wrong
Who said you shadowed Ireland's star,
Nor gave you laurel wreath nor song.
You proved by death as true as they,
In mightier conflicts played your part,
Equal your sacrifice may weigh,
Dear Kettle, of the generous heart.[45]

But the tide of violence was running too strongly for AE's pacific views to get a hearing, much less to make converts. With the ending of the world war and the beginning of the military struggle in Ireland, life became more insecure than ever. By a strange irony, one of the casualties of this new development was the co-operative movement. The creameries established with such loving care were taken by the Black-and-Tans to be nurseries of subversion and many were destroyed. In the *Irish Homestead* AE protested repeatedly but vainly against this mindless destruction, and, when in 1922 there came the ultimate disaster of civil war, his optimism, hitherto unquenchable, at last began to waver. 'In the shadows in Ireland, north and south,' he wrote in February, 'lurks reptilian human life, bigots who in the name of Christ spit on his precepts and who have put on the whole armoury of hate, men, and women too, who have known the dark intoxication of blood, and who seek half unconsciously for the renewal of that sinister ecstasy.'[46] It was about this time, also, that he suggested, by no means in jest, that someone should write a play 'about how the generations for 700 years fought for the liberation of beautiful Cathleen ni Houlihan, and when they set her free she walked out, a vituperative old hag'.[47]

Plunkett, that other pillar of the Anglo-Irish tradition, was less sensitive and more tenacious. As the old, measurable world collapsed around him, he busied himself with plans for the

[45] Reproduced in Henry Summerfield, *That Myriad Minded Man: a Biography of George William Russell, "A.E.", 1867–1935* (Gerrard's Cross, 1975), pp. 186–7.

[46] Ibid., p. 208.

[47] Ibid., p. 209.

redemption of the new, unknown one. His idea of a moderate reform party to work for dominion status could not take root at such a violent time, but he did succeed in launching another journal, the *Irish Statesman*, in 1919. In its original form it ran only for a year—it was to be brilliantly revived with AE as editor between 1923 and 1930—but even in that short space it gave an opportunity which hardly existed anywhere else to restate the Anglo-Irish position.

It was a position that had to be restated in the context of the partition of Ireland and of the consequent cutting off of the Anglo-Irish Protestants of the south, not only from the Protestants of the north, but also from the English connection which for so long had been their last line of defence. The debate about the future of this southern minority began almost simultaneously with the Anglo-Irish war. As early as November 1919, John Eglinton saw it for what it was at bottom, a question of nationality. 'To the ordinary Irish Protestant,' he wrote, 'Irish nationality seems now either a more or less seditious propaganda, or a kind of wild oats sown by his own community in its earlier days in the seventeenth and eighteenth centuries. To the Ulster Protestant, the phrase is stultified by its failure to include himself. To the Sinn Féiner it seems to represent more and more an entity which is gradually purging itself of its contamination since the age of Henry VIII through the interference of a crew of God-damned heretics . . . To the moderate Anglo-Irish, on the other hand, whether Protestant or Catholic, Irish nationality is a unifying influence, which must continue to proceed from them as it originated amongst them . . .'[48]

This bold claim, that the Anglo-Irish should again seize the leadership they had exercised in the eighteenth century, not only ignored everything that had happened since then, but also rested on a perverse view of that century. The nationalism which they had articulated at the time of Grattan had been a colonial nationalism, the nationalism of a strictly limited company from which the great majority of Irishmen had been excluded. Now the position was exactly reversed. Nevertheless, Eglinton believed that there

[48] *Irish Statesman*, 29 Nov. 1919.

was still an opportunity for an Anglo-Irish resurgence. Sinn Féin might be in a majority, and their view of nationality might be, as he put it, 'warped intellectually and tinged with obscurantism'. But at least the emergence of that formidable movement might force the apathetic Anglo-Irish to realize that 'there is nothing for it but to affirm Irish nationality'. 'The true destiny of Ireland', he declared, 'is to be a composite nationality.'[49]

The difficulty about this argument was that it begged the whole question of what it meant to be Anglo-Irish in the twentieth century, or indeed whether the term any longer had an exact meaning. The Anglo-Irish themselves, as we have seen, had seldom troubled to analyse their pedigree, being content simply to regard themselves as Irish. Now that claim was increasingly being called in question, and when a young Sinn Féin writer, P. S. O'Hegarty, attacked Eglinton on the ground that there was no such thing in the Ireland of 1919 as an Anglo-Irishman, he touched a tender nerve. 'There is a term, Anglo-Irish', he conceded, 'which is used, as a matter of convenience, to label Irish literature in the English language, but that is its sole significance. Anglo-Ireland died, or rather was strangled, in 1800 by its progenitor, because it was ceasing to be Anglo-Ireland and was becoming Ireland. It had either to do that or to become England.'[50] O'Hegarty's own viewpoint was, of course, coloured by the new cultural nationalism to which the Gaelic League had given such a stimulus. The nation, he insisted, had assimilated all newcomers, so that there was no such thing as a pure Gael any more than there was such a thing as an unadulterated Anglo-Irishman. The unifying factor was language, 'for the permanence of an Irish nation depends upon the attainment by that nation of a distinctive nationality'. 'Situated between England, with forty millions of English speakers, and North America, with a hundred millions, Ireland

[49] *Irish Statesman*, 27 Dec. 1919.

[50] Compare Thomas MacDonagh's definition, in *Literature in Ireland* (Dublin, 1916), p. 28. 'Here it is well at once to make clear that the term Anglo-Irish literature is applied very rarely to the meagre writings of the planters; it is worth having as a term only to apply to the literature produced by the English-speaking Irish, and by these in general only when writing in Ireland and for the Irish people.'

must either build upon the Irish language or become English.'[51]

These bleak alternatives were no more palatable to Eglinton in 1920 than when they had first been posed a generation earlier. On the one hand, he had no wish to be cut off from English culture. And on the other hand, as a Protestant dissenter, he had no desire to be engulfed by Sinn Féin, which he regarded as the manifestation of a Catholic Ireland that was in danger of imitating the exclusivism of the Protestant ascendancy of the eighteenth century. For him, not only did the Anglo-Irish exist, but they had a definite function. 'I see them . . .,' he replied, 'as a race of men who are in the mainstream of the Irish destiny, who have imposed their language and culture on Ireland, and have given it whatever degree of political unity it possesses—though I confess that is not a very high degree.'[52]

But the times were too much out of joint for such an argument to strike any answering chord in the minds of men who were at that moment asserting and imposing their own view of nationality by the bomb and the bullet. This was a fact of life which even Eglinton could not ignore indefinitely and in the end, just at the moment when the *Irish Statesman* was closing down in the summer of 1920, he advised his fellow-Protestants to abandon for the present any hope of unifying Ireland. A country, to achieve unity, must be capable of being regenerated and this capability he did not find in Ireland 'where an unreasoning deference to the past has precluded the emancipation of its spirit in religion, literature, or in political patriotism . . .'[53]

With the signing of the Anglo-Irish Treaty in 1921 and the launching of the Irish Free State along the perilous road of independence, or partial independence, it might well have seemed that for the former Protestant ascendancy, the rest would be silence. Yet it soon appeared that the founders of the state, Arthur Griffith and Kevin O'Higgins in particular, were anxious to allay the natural fears of the southern unionists and, provided

[51] P. S. O'Hegarty, 'The Anglo-Irish Affirmation of Nationality', in *Irish Statesman*, 31 Jan. 1920.
[52] *Irish Statesman*, 7 Feb. 1920.
[53] *Irish Statesman*, 19 June 1920.

they gave unquestioned allegiance to the new regime, to integrate them as far as possible into the structure of government. Griffith undertook, when setting up the upper house or Senate of the Irish legislature, to ensure reasonable representation for minority interests, and in his nominations for thirty out of the sixty seats in the first Senate, he gave great prominence to the surviving Anglo-Irish. Sixteen of the thirty were identifiable as archetypal southern unionists, but these included men like Lord Dunraven, Lord Mayo, and Sir William Hutcheson-Poë, who in the early years of the century had all played an important part in bringing the land question to a satisfactory solution. They included, also, men of business like the distiller, Andrew Jameson, and H. S. Guinness, both of them directors of the Bank of Ireland, and Sir Nugent Everard, one of the leading advocates of Irish industrial development. Among the other new senators were Sir Horace Plunkett; the writer and surgeon, Oliver Gogarty; and, most remarkable of all, the poet Yeats who chose this moment to make his grand gesture of returning to live in Dublin.[54]

This seemed evidence of benevolent intent, and, though it fell short of what the southern unionists themselves had hoped for, they accepted it with a good grace, realizing that the government had made a deliberate effort to bring them within the frontier of the new nation. And even though Griffith died before he could see his experiment in action, Kevin O'Higgins, perhaps the ablest surviving member of the administration, reaffirmed the policy of reconciliation in words that indicated a real desire not to wreak vengeance upon those who had belonged to a different but defeated tradition. 'We being the majority and strength of the country . . . it comes well from us to make a generous adjustment to show that these people are regarded, not as alien enemies, not as planters, but that we regarded them as part and parcel of this nation, and that we wish them to take their share of its responsibilities.'[55]

In my final lecture I shall try to show how this noble sentiment fared when set beside the reality of life in a divided island.

[54] Donal O'Sullivan, *The Irish Free State and its Senate* (London, 1940), pp. 90–1.
[55] Dáil Éireann, debates, i. 242.

5

Ulster: the Roots of Difference

It will be remembered that whenever President de Gaulle wished to commune with his soul he withdrew to his country estate at Colombey les Deux Églises. So also Captain Terence O'Neill (as he then was), when prime minister of Northern Ireland, would sometimes leave the hurly-burly of Belfast and seek refuge at his ancestral home in the little town of Ahoghill. The parallel did not escape the wits and before long Ahoghill was rechristened Ahoghill les Trois Églises. Like most Ulster jokes this one has a sting in its tail. That single phrase, 'les trois églises', reminds us not only of the co-existence of three local cultures within the context of the dominant English culture, but also that these three cultures were embedded in three different varieties of religion— Anglican, Presbyterian, and Roman Catholic.

This confronts us immediately with the question any Irishman is likely to be asked nowadays when the subject of Northern Ireland comes up. It is a question that is usually phrased in one of two ways. Either it is said, 'If people behave towards each other as they are now doing in Ulster, how can they be said to be doing so in the name of religion, as that word is generally understood in civilized countries?' Or else it is said, 'Since in this day and age people do not generally get killed for their religious beliefs, is it not the case that "Protestant" and "Catholic" are simply a convenient shorthand to describe conflicts of interest at some other, perhaps more profound, level?'

Both these questions fail to encompass the complexity of the Ulster question. While it is perfectly true that the religious labels do mask other conflicts of interest, it is not true that such conflicts would be regarded by many who are caught up in them as more 'profound' than the religious differences which divide them. Nor is it true that the savagery of the present conflict is necessarily incompatible with genuine religious feeling: on the contrary, the history of religion has produced too many examples of fanaticism in action for us to accept uncritically the notion that love and charity are the only modes in which piety expresses itself. But, it may be objected, in Britain religious rivalry has at least not taken the form of open warfare since the seventeenth century. Why should Northern Ireland be the exception? It would be tempting but unprofitable to repeat the glib answer which this question often evokes—that the seventeenth century has not yet ended there. For while, in a certain sense—the highly important mythic sense to which I must presently return—this may be true, that only moves our question one stage further back. We have to rephrase it something like this. 'If the spectre of the seventeenth century is omnipresent in Northern Ireland, how can this be so, and to what extent has its continuing influence been affected by other developments since then?'

Even that formulation does not take us far enough into the tangled past. To elucidate the clash of cultures in modern Ulster we shall have to adopt a different method of inquiry from that used in earlier lectures. It was possible then to describe the conflict between Irish Ireland and Anglo-Irish Ireland in terms of a sharp, decisive engagement fought out over a limited period and largely concentrated in a single place. This was partly because Dublin, as the capital city, was an obvious battle-ground and partly because the supposed vacuum caused by the Parnellite split allowed the generation that grew up in the shadow of that event to turn away from politics, if only for a while. But in Ulster the same considerations did not apply. The Parnellite split made much less impact there and in any event Belfast could not, indeed did not, aspire to play the same role as Dublin. In the north, therefore, the collision between cultures took a different form, in some ways more diffuse, in others more intense. We shall not find a brightly-lit stage on which the writers and the scholars engage in highly stylized personal combat. Instead, we shall be concerned with a situation where political antagonisms never cease to be strongly marked, but where the roots of difference are so deeply buried that we can only uncover them by exploring large tracts of time. That is why it is necessary to stress the importance of the seventeenth century, but also why it is equally necessary not to lay the blame for all modern dissensions upon that century. On the contrary, we shall see that some features of Ulster which go back to the beginning of history, or even to prehistory, are still relevant at the present day. That this antique evidence sometimes seems to point us in opposite directions simply underlines the central fact about Ulster, that it has always experienced a double pull—towards the rest of Ireland, and also towards the larger island. The point has been best expressed by Professor Estyn Evans, the geographer who has done so much to extend our knowledge of the subject. 'The visitor to Northern Ireland,' he has written, 'must not expect to find here a mere provincial variation of the land of Britain: he will discover a land and a people of strong personality, in some ways more British than the British, yet in other ways more Irish than the Irish.'[1]

This dual character of the province is of the utmost significance, reappearing as it does at every stage in its history. Being the nearest part of the island to the 'mainland', it was a point of entry for the early inhabitants of the country. The traffic across the narrow bridge between what became Ireland and what became Scotland has passed in *both* directions on many subsequent occasions and always it has reinforced the lessons of geography and geology, that Ireland was an extension of an entity much bigger than itself. To quote Professor Evans again: 'The land that was to become Ireland . . . may be said to have been held in a pincer grip between the converging western ends of two ancient mountain systems which also embrace Great Britain.'[2] Not only was the geological configuration of Ulster closest to that of the 'mainland', but the region was also separated from the rest of Ireland by a natural barrier of small hills (drumlins), forests, bogs,

---

[1] E. Estyn Evans, *Northern Ireland: a Portrait* (London, 1951), p. 7.
[2] E. Estyn Evans, *The Personality of Ireland* (Cambridge, 1973), p. 21; see also Frank Mitchell, *The Irish Landscape* (London, 1976), pp. 114–17.

lakes, and water-courses. Behind this barrier there developed a region differentiated from others by its climate, its geology and its human geography.

Does such differentiation mean that Ulster has remained closer to Scotland—with which, both as colonizer and as colony, its ties have always been intimate—than to the rest of Ireland? Some have indeed argued so, but the assumption is hardly justified by the evidence.[3] Professor Evans, placing Ulster firmly within what he calls 'the essential unity of Ireland', has described it as a 'strong regional variant in habitat, heritage and history', and that, perhaps, is the most balanced view available to us.[4] But from it we may draw the paradoxical conclusion that precisely because of its isolation, the region in some ways retained more of the ancient past of the country than other areas which were more easily over-run. Thus, the old Gaelic civilization actually found its last stronghold in Ulster.

That Gaelic civilization had, of course, come under repeated pressure even in Ulster after the arrival of the Normans in the twelfth century, but it was not substantially displaced until the seventeenth century, which is why that century remains the hinge upon which turns much of the modern history of the region. Several facts are relevant here. First, we have always to remember that the conquest was long-drawn-out and uncertain and that what was begun in Tudor times was only completed a couple of decades before the Hanoverians came in. Secondly, we have to realize that it was not a total conquest, in the sense that the previous inhabitants were wiped out. On the contrary, they either retreated to the harsher mountain land, or to the poorer stretches of the lowlands, often continuing as tenants, or later even as labourers, on soil where their ancestors had once been supreme.

---

[3] M. W. Heslinga, *The Irish Border as a Cultural Divide* (Assen, 1971), pp. 100–1, would argue that the present land border between Northern Ireland and the Republic of Ireland marks an extension of the historic land border between Scotland and England. Because of similarities he observes between England and the Republic he regards this land boundary as a more absolute cultural divide than the Irish Sea. But this is a somewhat extreme view, not generally accepted.

[4] E. Estyn Evans, *The Personality of Ireland*, pp. 74, 82.

And finally, the conquest, such as it was, was identified almost from the beginning with religious enmity. This was partly because it became almost accidentally involved in the larger conflict between 'Protestant' and 'Catholic' in Europe, but still more because it occurred at a moment when religious attitudes seemed to be hardening everywhere. Three creeds therefore collided in Ulster—a triumphant and arrogant Anglicanism, a rigid post-Tridentine Catholicism, and a Calvinism which had begun to settle into strict orthodoxy by the time the Presbyterians appeared in Ulster in significant numbers.

The tensions between these creeds would in any event have been considerable, but they were greatly heightened by the fact that the conquest was for so long balanced on a knife-edge. The English and Scottish settlers were acutely vulnerable to a counter-attack—especially in West Ulster where they were thin on the ground—and in 1641 the long-dreaded native insurrection came at last. Largely motivated by the determination of the dispossessed to regain their land, the uprising also had strong religious overtones, so much so that the 'massacre' of 1641 passed into Protestant mythology as a kind of St Bartholomew so quickly that within ten years Cromwell was using it to justify his own massacre of the Irish at Drogheda.[5] The importance of this episode, exaggerated in the telling though it seems to have been almost from the moment that it happened, in helping to create the siege mentality of the Ulster Protestant can scarcely be over-rated. 'Like an unseen planet whose presence is revealed only by its influence on other celestial bodies,' a modern historian has written, 'the rebellion betrays its significance in later events: the more one explores Ulster history, the more one becomes aware of its occult force. Sooner or later in each successive crisis, the cry is raised of "1641 come again".'[6] And when to this is added that other symbolic event—the siege of Derry in 1689 by the forces of James II—then it becomes easier to understand the underlying fear

[5] A. T. Q. Stewart, *The Narrow Ground: Aspects of Ulster 1609–1969* (London, 1977), pp. 45–52; Lady Antonia Fraser, *Cromwell our Chief of Men* (London, 1973), pp. 327–40.

[6] A. T. Q. Stewart, op. cit., p. 49.

and insecurity which have been at the root of so much Protestant aggressiveness since the seventeenth century.

To represent the conflict of religions simply as one between Catholics and Protestants is, however, to over-simplify. Scarcely less significant was the clash of Anglican with Presbyterian, a clash which was not merely religious, but also one of class and, in the broadest sense, of culture. The Anglican ascendancy in Ulster as elsewhere was primarily an ascendancy of parsons and land-owners. The latter may have begun humbly enough as Jacobean planters or Cromwellian settlers, but the ownership of land soon worked its accustomed magic and, although there were always some who remained at the bottom of the social ladder, by the eighteenth century the Anglicans were emerging as the gentry of the province, often on a considerable scale. By 1800 there were in Ulster over 300 estates of more than 2,000 acres each and a quarter of these exceeded 10,000 acres.[7] Such landlords did not differ significantly from the inheritors of the Revolution settle-ment in other parts of Ireland, intermarrying with them and, after they had risen in the world, even with greater families in England. And since the central power was far away in Dublin, they were, and felt themselves to be, an active governing class, their suprem-acy based partly on property and partly on the penal laws which, though in some respects laxly administered, denied to Catholics, and to a lesser extent to Presbyterians, the civil rights necessary to full citizenship.

Even after the Penal Laws had vanished, even after the Irish parliament was extinguished in 1800, the dominance of the Anglo-Irish gentry over Ulster society remained virtually un-challenged. True, as the nineteenth century drew to its close, their economic base was weakened, first by the Famine, next by the land war, and then by the land legislation. On the other hand, the necessity for Protestants to hang together in face of Catholic and nationalist pressures, gave them a larger political importance than any their southern brethren could aspire to, and this in turn reinforced their social leadership. It was noticeable, for

[7] R. B. McDowell, 'The Landed Classes and the Professions', in T. W. Moody and J. C. Beckett (ed.), *Ulster Since 1800* (second series, London, 1957), p. 99.

example, that in the last quarter of the nineteenth century the Orange Order, which had been languishing for fifty years as a not very respectable and decidedly plebeian organization, was taken up once more by the gentry and in consequence became much more widely representative of Protestant attitudes and classes.

Yet the gentry themselves remained embedded in the Anglo-Irish tradition and the pattern of their lives changed little from generation to generation. Public school in England was followed most often by service in the armed forces of the Crown, though for the eldest son this would eventually be interrupted when his turn came to assume the responsibilities of ownership. These included both county government and the administration of justice in the magistrates courts, as well as the maintenance of family estates and houses. Leadership of society in a province where religious observance was intense meant that they also took a prominent part in parish and diocesan affairs. It was, for example, not unusual for a man such as Colonel Edward Saunderson, who in the early years of the twentieth century was both leader of the Ulster Unionist M.P.s and Grand Master of the Orange Order, to take the service in the absence of his rector and even on occasion to preach the sermon.

The Anglicanism professed by Saunderson and his like was strongly marked by the evangelicalism typical of the nineteenth-century Church of Ireland and this was perhaps something which separated them from the gentlemen of England whom, outwardly at least, they so much resembled. But they did not think of themselves as other than Irish. Many of their families had been rooted in the Ulster countryside since the seventeenth century. They knew its history, cherished its antiquities, loved each feature of its landscape, worked, for the most part easily, with its people. Yet, though Ulster was dear to them, and they felt it to be their special place, they saw it ultimately in a British context. For the Lenox-Conynghams, for instance, who had been in the province for three hundred years, service in the British Army was as inevitable as breathing, as it was for the O'Neills and McCalmonts, or the Hamiltons and Stewarts, or the Brookes and

Archdales, or for a hundred other families. Loyalty to the Crown, loyalty to their province, distrust of Catholics, were all confusedly locked together in their minds. And when Mina Lowry, who married into the Lenox-Conyngham family and wrote their history in *An Old Ulster House*, came to describe her own experiences, she found no incongruity in grouping together within a few pages a semi-regal visit from Sir Edward Carson, a review of the Ulster Volunteers in the neighbourhood of a 'dangerous and disloyal' (i.e. Catholic) village, and the flocking of Ulstermen to the colours in August 1914. Her book ends with the house returning to normal after American occupation in the Second World War. What, she asked herself, was the secret of its spell? Her answer was quintessentially Anglo-Irish. 'It is difficult to say; but we like to remember the evening sunlight slanting through tall trees where jackdaws chatter, and making flickering patterns on walls hung with portraits, from which many a former occupant looks mysteriously down. A strange peace pervades these quiet rooms and one feels that the leading characteristic of Springhill is that of an old home, dearly loved and stored with relics and memories of by-gone days.'[8]

This excursion into nostalgia gives us an important clue to the innate love of the Anglo-Irish for their estates and their province. But there is an apt symbolism in the fact that Mrs Lenox-Conyngham should have sung the praises of a house, for it was in building that the Anglo-Irish left their chief mark upon Ulster. Little, indeed, has survived from the original settlements. The 'English' black and white timber and plaster houses of the Lagan Valley were virtually wiped out in 1641 and of the houses which lined the frontier—the 'bawns' or farmhouses protected by battlements and towers—the survivors today are mostly ruins. The early churches, built in a style later christened Planters' Gothic, also disappeared for the most part in the seventeenth century. They too had a fortress-like appearance, the visible expression of that siege mentality which is never far from Ulster Protestantism. Relying usually on the local skills of mason, carpenter, and

---

[8] Mina Lenox-Conyngham, *An Old Ulster House* (Dundalk, 1946), pp. 219–22, 242.

blacksmith, they were churches with little decoration and without any pretension save to provide, as has been said, 'an architecture of congregational worship'.[9] However, with the more settled times after 1690, Ulster shared in the Georgian efflorescence and Palladian influences, in particular, made themselves felt in a number of great houses around Belfast and in some more isolated mansions—for example Florencecourt or Castlecoole. At a less splendid level, Georgian Ulster abounded in the wide streets and 'diamonds' (squares) of the prosperous country towns, with their neat brick terraces of admirably proportioned houses; the same tradition of shapeliness was to be found alike in plain, substantial farm-houses and in the now rare but beautiful oval thatched cottages.[10]

Yet, if this Anglo-Irish culture dictated much (though by no means all) of the physical appearance of most of Ulster, and if the gentry preserved a governing role there longer than in the rest of Ireland, we look in vain for any comparable contribution to the intellect or the imagination of the province. Apart from the coterie that revolved round Bishop Thomas Percy of Dromore (Percy of the *Reliques of Ancient English Poetry*) at the end of the eighteenth century, there is little to catch the eye. And the Percy coterie, it must be said, amounts only to a small protuberance in an exceedingly flat plain. A limpet-like attachment to Augustan platitude seems to have been their distinguishing characteristic, as this brief but typical extract from Thomas Stott's *The Songs of Deardra* will show:

> How fair the peopled district round *Dromore*!
> Here wealth and comfort industry supplies;
> While vales extend, enrich'd with flaxen store,
> And hills adorn'd by cultivation rise.

These Anglo-Irish Augustans were before long to be over-shadowed by the romanticism of which Percy's *Reliques* was itself a harbinger, but little of the Ossianic poetry which drew on such

[9] D. O'D. Hanna, 'Architecture in Ulster' in S. Hanna Bell, Nesca A. Robb, and John Hewitt (ed.), *The Arts in Ulster* (London, 1951), p. 34.
[10] Ibid., pp. 25–44.

natural features of the province as the Giant's Causeway, showed much real feeling for landscape or topography, or for people. Nor did the nineteenth century add much to the sum of Anglo-Irish literary culture, unless we except William Allingham who was much praised by Yeats, but who was, like so many of Yeats's swans, indisputably a minor poet. Not until the twentieth century did they find in Louis MacNeice a voice to speak for them, though then it was to express not their former confident certainties, but their modern predicament. And even MacNeice belonged not to the gentry proper, but to the Church of Ireland middle class:

> I was the rector's son, born to the Anglican order,
> Banned for ever from the candles of the Irish poor.[11]

Banned also, he might have added, from the innermost circle of the ascendancy, both by reason of his almost permanent exile in England and because whenever Ulster became his theme, as from time to time it did compulsively, he cast an equally cold eye upon Protestant and upon Catholic, as in *Autumn Journal*:

> Why should I want to go back
> To you, Ireland, my Ireland?
> The blots on the page are so black
> That they cannot be covered with shamrock.
> I hate your grandiose airs,
> Your sob-stuff, your laugh and your swagger,
> Your assumption that everyone cares
> Who is the king of your castle.
> Castles are out of date,
> The tide flows round the children's sandy fancy;
> Put up what flag you like, it is too late
> To save your soul with bunting.
> *Odi atque amo:*
> Shall we cut this name on trees with a rusty dagger?
> Her mountains are still blue, her rivers flow
> Bubbling over the boulders

[11] Cited in T. Brown, *Northern Voices: Poets from Ulster* (Dublin and London, 1975), p. 15.

She is both a bore and a bitch;
Better close the horizon,
Send her no more fantasy, no more longings which
Are under a fatal tariff.
For common sense is the vogue
And she gives her children neither sense nor money
Who slouch around the world with a gesture and a brogue
And a faggot of useless memories.

It is relevant to recall that MacNeice's attitude to Ireland was shaped by a childhood spent in an atmosphere of narrow and oppressive Puritanism. In an autobiographical fragment, *The Strings are False*, he remembers the poverty by which the comfortable family home was surrounded, and the circumambient fear and hatred which combined to form the 'neolithic night' that recurs constantly in his Irish poetry.[12] The particular Puritanism which he experienced was the Puritanism of evangelical Anglicanism, but in spirit and in style it was not far different from the Puritanism of the Presbyterian ethic. There was, however, a fundamental social distinction between them upon which a no less fundamental cultural difference was based. This was that Anglicanism operated mainly at the two extremes of the class spectrum. It was, and it still remains, the religion of the old county families. But it had also been the religion of many English yeomen who settled on the land. When Belfast became industrialized in the nineteenth century, a number of the descendants of these yeomen moved into the city, bringing their Anglicanism with them, and their numbers were swelled by the missionary zeal of the Church of Ireland among the factory population. Presbyterianism, on the other hand, though deeply rooted in the countryside of eastern Ulster, was reinforced even before the end of the seventeenth century by craftsmen and weavers, English as well as Scottish, who were among the first accumulators of capital, albeit on a modest scale. From their ranks came the early entrepreneurs of industrialism and during the nineteenth century

[12] Michael Longley, 'The Neolithic Night: a Note on the Irishness of Louis MacNeice' in Douglas Dunn (ed.), *Two Decades of Irish Writing*, pp. 98–104.

they emerged as the dominant force, not only in the business life of Belfast, but in its social and cultural life as well.

This dominance was built upon a Scottish connection reaching much further back than the plantation of 1606 and its successors. We have already seen that from earliest times there had been a traffic between Ulster and Scotland which moved in both directions. Between the fourteenth and the sixteenth centuries that part of Ulster which lay nearest to Scotland—Antrim—had formed part of the lordship which the MacDonnells exercised over the Isles, and when their power was broken in Scotland, Antrim still remained their base up to the end of the Tudor period. This lordship was an important link between Gaelic Scotland and Gaelic Ireland and was certainly a factor in strengthening Gaelic influences in north-east Ulster. However, with the accession of James I and the beginning of a deliberate policy of colonization, a new and ultimately far more powerful strain was added to the Scottish element. The process of immigration was not confined, either in date or in place, to the original plantation, but continued at intervals throughout the seventeenth century and especially in its second half. It was most heavily concentrated in the eastern part of Ulster, where there had been settlement of one kind or another for many centuries and where so many layers of population were already intermingled that, as has been well said, 'there never was any true confrontation of archetypal Planter and Gael'.[13] This confused situation was perpetuated by a considerable movement of Presbyterians out of Ulster (to America and elsewhere) towards the end of the eighteenth century. Driven partly by economic pressures, and partly by resentment at their continued exclusion from full civil rights, they ensured by their departure that whatever hope there might once have been that Presbyterians would dominate the province numerically would have to be abandoned. It was not long after this that the familiar triangular balance of Anglicans, Presbyterians, and Roman Catholics began to emerge.

Nevertheless, the influx of the seventeenth century was decisive in one all-important sense. It injected into Ulster that

[13] A. T. Q. Stewart, *The Narrow Ground*, p. 41.

uncompromising Calvinism which was to influence so much of its subsequent history. These Presbyterians brought with them a characteristic tendency towards individualism and heterodoxy, both in matters of doctrine and of organization. This produced in the eighteenth century a schism between those who favoured subscription to the Westminster Confession of Faith of 1643 and those who were against it. There was also a further split between the orthodox of the Synod (the governing body of the church since 1690) and those who formally seceded from what they regarded as an excessively centralized structure: the seceders themselves then rapidly split into other sub-sections. These quarrels continued into the nineteenth century when they were dramatized by the personal conflict between two leading divines —Henry Montgomery and the formidable Henry Cooke, the 'Presbyterian Pope' as his opponents called him. Essentially, it was a battle between liberalism and conservatism, and the latter, in the person of Henry Cooke, triumphed, though at the cost of further secessions. This victory of the so-called 'Old Light' over the 'New Light' meant, in broad terms, the deliberate adoption by a majority of Presbyterians of an unequivocally evangelical stance. It marked, as a modern historian has said, 'the choice of grace and faith and revelation in place of the seeming alternative of law and logic; it was a conscious suffrage cast for God and religion rather than for man and his speculations'.[14]

This settlement not only paved the way for a reconciliation with the earlier seceders and the creation in 1840 of the General Assembly of the Presbyterian Church in Ireland, it came in good time to prepare the soil for the 'great revival' of 1859. This extraordinary movement was not confined to Ulster, and it affected all the major denominations, but in its full vigour it was primarily an Ulster Presbyterian phenomenon. Like most such episodes in the history of religious hysteria, its origin, propagation, and eventual decline seemed incapable of rational explanation, except perhaps in terms of a mass hunger for salvation by congregations oppressed in spirit by a too rigid application of the doctrine of election. Whatever the root cause, the records of the

[14] J. E. Davey, *1840–1940, the Story of a Hundred Years* (Belfast, 1940), p. 10.

time are full of accounts of seizures, mass conversions, even in some places cases of possession or the appearance of stigmata. This contemporary account from Dundrod in county Antrim gives something of the chaotic excitement which the revival could generate in a small community:

When I visited the district I found that all labour was completely superseded, and that all the people were running in groups from house to house . . . In some houses at one time I counted more than a score, old and young, more or less affected. The people here seemed to 'take it' with wonderful rapidity. The graveyard is filled with groups singing and praying around the prostrate bodies of men and women. Some are as in a trance, others crying for mercy. Some are still falling into the arms of friends and sinking as into a swoon. Some stagger to a distance and drop on their knees to pray over the graves of the dead; and a few rush to the gates and flee in terror from the scene.[15]

It was perhaps significant that the revival seemed to arise spontaneously among ordinary men and women, with many ministers following reluctantly, having failed to control or suppress it. And for those who saw it as *The Year of Grace*, there were others who saw it as *The Year of Delusion*.[16] Yet, whether grace or delusion, it illustrated vividly an important element in Ulster Protestantism, whether Anglican or Presbyterian—the deep reserves of emotion which the normal conduct of their religion kept in strict restraint, but which, largely because of that restraint, could build up from time to time into explosions of violent feeling and action. This was to happen again only fifteen years later, with the visit to the province of the American evangelists, Moody and Sankey, and it is perhaps not very different from the more disciplined fervour which was so evident at the signing of the Solemn League and Covenant against Home Rule in 1912.

In religious terms, the great revival probably helped to strengthen certain existing tendencies in Ulster Presbyterianism. There was an evident increase in evangelism, in missionary work, and in preaching a gospel which was a universal message for all men. That gospel had still, of course, to be conformable to Calvinism, but there was less obsessive concern with doctrines

[15] Cited in J. W. Good, *Ulster and Ireland* (Dublin and London, 1919), pp. 116–17.

[16] These are the titles of two contemporary pamphlets dealing with the revival.

relating to 'effectual calling' and 'reprobation'. There was, too, an increased bias towards emotional preaching, leading perhaps to some retreat of reasoned argument in face of unscientific credulity. This in turn may not have been unconnected with another marked feature of evolving Presbyterianism, stimulated by Henry Cooke for his own ends—that is the increasing authority of laymen in the government of the Presbyterian Church in Ireland.

Older strands in Presbyterianism continued, however, to be important. The Puritan austerity that was evident from the earliest days of settlement persisted largely intact throughout the nineteenth century and is by no means dead in the twentieth. It was evident even in the architecture of their churches, once times had become settled enough for them to build with any hope of permanence. Their hall-mark was the so-called 'Barn' church, which, as the name implies, was a long, spare, rectangular shape, redeemed from plainness by its proportions, its fan-light entrance, its tall box-pews and occasional baroque pulpit. This style survived into the first half of the nineteenth century, modulating into an ornamented classicism sometimes called Post-Regency. It was a severe, restrained architecture which, significantly, was chiefly found among the non-subscribing congregations. And perhaps it is no less significant that when the Gothic revival afflicted the Presbyterian Church about the middle of the nineteenth century with an exuberance of red brick, it was the more evangelical wing that responded most eagerly to the new style, finding, perhaps, in its brash and over-emphatic earnestness a fitting frame for the Gothic oratory which rolled down from the pulpits each Sabbath day.

To speak of the Sabbath is to recall another feature of this severely disciplined faith. Ulster Presbyterianism was strict in its observance of the Lord's Day, regarding this as extending from six o'clock on Saturday evening to midnight on Sunday. In the most orthodox households no cooking was permitted and personal ablutions, even shaving, were left undone.[17] In its public

---

[17] Such strictness sooner or later rebounded. That sharp observer, the essayist Robert Lynd, noted early in the new century that Sunday had become 'the fullest

manifestations this rigorousness involved a closing down of virtually all amenities and sources of entertainment on the Sabbath day. The larger centres, Belfast especially, seemed totally deserted, save for the thronging crowds which attended church, sometimes more than once in the day, to hear sermons (often of a fundamentalist kind) lasting at least an hour, and expositions of scripture almost as lengthy. Nor was this felt to be a hardship, for the minister stood or fell in the judgement of his congregation largely by the quality and fervour (not always the same thing) of his pulpit oratory. The sermon was thus a major, perhaps the major, cultural experience shared by the whole community, something to be 'tasted' and discussed throughout the following week. Since devout households did not admit much profane literature, abominated cards and billiards, and looked askance at the theatre or, later, the cinema, the minister's only rivals were politicians' speeches, generally cast in a similar mould, the more solid newspapers, particularly the *Belfast Telegraph*, and the missionary and other magazines turned out in great profusion by the Presbyterian Church itself.

It followed as a matter of course that a heavy emphasis was put upon sobriety of dress and of behaviour, and still more upon temperance. Not all Presbyterians were total abstainers by any means—some of them were distillers of excellent whiskey—but social pressures operated strongly against any wide use of spirits, while conceding, at most, a moderate use of wine. Which kind of wine should be used in communion services was itself a burning issue and the General Assembly debated bitterly, for decade after decade, whether it should be from a fermented or an unfermented grape. Some congregations were so divided that they maintained two separate communion tables, though not many perhaps would have given the doctrine of election such an original twist as the layman who wrote: 'If Christ used fermented wine, he could not be my Saviour.'[18]

---

feeding-day of the week' (Robert Lynd, *Home Life in Ireland* (London, 1909), pp. 214–15).

[18] J. E. Davey, *1840–1940, the Story of a Hundred Years*, p. 58.

The emphasis upon abstinence and restraint also dictated that religious services should be serious and decorous occasions. Not only were church interiors kept to an almost ostentatious plainness, but the use of instrumental music was a stumbling-block to many, for although the voices of the congregation had been raised in song from the beginning, it had sufficed the first settlers to be given the lead by the precentor with his simple tuning-fork or tabor pipe. While his reign lasted, Henry Cooke had been able to arrest the march of modernity and it was not until the end of the nineteenth century that organs were generally admitted, though some congregations held out against them even after that. Similarly with the vexed question of hymn-singing. In the early days the Psalms alone, or with Scottish doxologies, had sufficed. But in the first half of the nineteenth century paraphrases began to be used in the Synod of Ulster, though not among the Seceders. After the great revival, when the emotional content of the services began to be greater, hymns were used so extensively that in 1899 Ulster and Scottish Presbyterians combined to produce a *Church Hymnary*; this, however, was optional and many congregations ignored it.

This simple culture was, for most of its adherents, a non-literary one which did not encourage either the reading or the writing of imaginative literature. In the latter part of the eighteenth century there had indeed been a brief emergence of poetry, composed mostly by weavers settled in Antrim and Down. They were influenced by the Bible, especially the Psalms, and also by a long-established Scots tradition culminating in the work of Robert Burns, which they may to some extent have anticipated or paralleled. The most notable of them, James Orr (1778–1816), not only wrote his best work in Central Scots dialect, but even included among his poems an 'Irish Cottar's Death and Burial', which is close to Burns in spirit as well as in content and some would say superior in both.[19] It has been suggested by the modern Ulster poet, John Hewitt, that these weaver poets represented, in effect, a regional variant of a larger folk-culture, preceding Burns but also in due course embracing

[19] T. Brown, *Northern Voices*, pp. 5–14.

him, whose homeland was the Scottish lowlands.[20] If so, the Scottish influence was persistent, for as late as the beginning of the twentieth century, the Ulster writer, Lynn Doyle, was introduced to Burns's work by the ploughman on the farm where he grew up.[21] But this fragile rural art was not built to withstand the triple shock that shattered it during the nineteenth century. First, individuality was driven underground by a national school system which aimed at a Benthamite ideal of efficient uniformity (or mediocrity). Next, the Famine, though less severe in Ulster than in other regions (except West Ulster, which suffered badly), helped to loosen the ancient ties that had bound the countryman to his daily labour and had given him a sense of place. And finally, overlapping the Famine, came the industrial revolution, which drew into the Lagan Valley much of the population uprooted from the land. Social and cultural values were increasingly determined there by a Presbyterian middle class with one eye firmly fixed on God and the other as firmly fixed on Mammon, and imbued with the determination to live honest, sober lives from which anything resembling art for art's sake would be rigorously excluded.[22]

Not surprisingly, the Puritan virtues flowed into other channels. To the extent that they expressed themselves intellectually, they did so in theology, law, history, medicine, and science. Few novels, little poetry, hardly any drama, attract the eye until the beginning of the twentieth century. This was not due so much to lack of talent, as to lack of interest and, more particularly, to lack of patronage. Thus, although Belfast, like Dublin, was on the itinerary of visiting companies and celebrities from London, it provided few incentives for its own artists who had scarcely any option but to go elsewhere. Among painters this was true of Sir John Lavery, of Charles Lamb, of Paul Henry, and later of Daniel O'Neill, George Campbell, and William Scott.[23] Among

[20] John Hewitt (ed.), *Rhyming Weavers* (Belfast, 1974), pp. 1–6.

[21] Lynn Doyle, *An Ulster Childhood* (Dublin and London, 1921), pp. 12–21.

[22] For a contemporary view, see F. Frankfort Moore, *The Truth about Ulster* (London, 1914), especially chap. 9.

[23] On the credit side may be set two exceptional artists who stood their ground—William Conor (1881–1968), painter of mill girls and shipyard workers,

musicians it was true also of Charles Wood, Hamilton Harty, and Herbert Hughes. And among writers it was true of William Carleton, AE, Shan Bullock, Robert Lynd, Joseph Campbell, J. H. Cousins, and others. The few writers who were active in the province in the late nineteenth and early twentieth centuries and who managed to liberate themselves from English vogues and models were mostly secondary figures who either subordinated their art to political purposes or else indulged in idealized, pastoral versions of the heroic legends or of contemporary peasant life. Among the former were Alice Milligan (1866–1953) and Ethna Carbery (1886–1911, born Anna Johnston and later married to the Donegal novelist, Seamus MacManus), both of whom became deeply involved in the Irish Ireland movement, founding in Belfast in the early 1890s the periodical, *Shan Van Vocht* ('The Poor Old Woman', a traditional symbol of Ireland) which anticipated Griffith's *United Irishman* and was eventually absorbed by it. Of the more strictly pastoral poets, Moira O'Neill (1864–1955), a product of the ascendancy, was perhaps the most popular in her day. Only one poet at that time, Richard Rowley (1887–1947, in private life Richard Valentine Williams), seriously confronted the phenomenon of Belfast. Despite his limitations, which were many, Rowley could occasionally—as, for example, in *City Songs* (1918) and *Workers* (1923) break through to a realization that the city was not only harsh and powerful, but also, in its brooding way, beautiful.

The one towering exception to this catalogue of naïve indigenes was the novelist, Forrest Reid (1876–1947), who, apart from his Cambridge education, lived and wrote nearly all his life in and around his native Belfast. But he belonged to a more cosmopolitan tradition and his friend, E. M. Forster, knew how isolated he really was. 'He was', Forster once wrote, 'the most important man in Belfast, and though it would be too much to say that Belfast knew him not, I have sometimes smiled to think how

---

and Colin Middleton (b. 1910), an artist of immense versatility, energy, and achievement.

little that great city, engaged in its own ponderous purposes, dreamed of him, or indeed of anything.'[24]

Only in the theatre did something new and peculiar to the province emerge before the establishment of Northern Ireland in 1920 and even this arose out of the Irish literary revival in Dublin. Originally, it was the intention of a few amateur enthusiasts to found a branch of the Irish Literary Theatre in Belfast. Somewhat coldly received by the parent body, they formed their own organization, the Ulster Literary Theatre, in 1904. Some of the founding members, for example Bulmer Hobson, had dreamt of using the new movement as a vehicle for propagating the ideas of Sinn Féin, but most of those who wrote for the theatre were more concerned to express what they called the 'Ulster genius', which they took to be satiric. Only gradually did they produce Ulster plays and at first these were strongly influenced by Yeats's experiments in verse. From about 1905, however, there began to appear a homely, rustic drama depicting Ulster men and women in ordinary situations and using everyday speech. This kind of drama reflected something inherent in the character of the province, the down-to-earth temperament of the Ulsterman, and out of it came a distinctive art form—the 'kitchen comedy' of which Rutherford Mayne, George Shiels, St John Ervine, and Lynn Doyle were the leading exponents. Yet even this lively theatre existed only on the margin of Belfast life. It was not affluent enough to offer a reasonable living to its actors and dramatists, and although it survived precariously until the 1930s, when it was succeeded by the Ulster Group Theatre, it never had a building of its own and was confined to short seasons at the Opera House or in makeshift halls whenever it could find them, interspersed with tours to Dublin or London. Not surprisingly, many of its dramatists and actors followed the musicians and painters and writers into exile.[25]

[24] Cited in S. Hanna Bell, Nesca A. Robb, and John Hewitt (ed.), *The Arts in Ulster*, p. 115. See also John Hewitt's comment that although Reid was the only Ulster writer of high quality in his generation to remain in the province, 'his exile from us was more absolute than that of any who left our borders or shores' (John Hewitt, 'Writing in Ulster', in *The Bell*, vol. xviii, no. 4 (July 1952), p. 20).

[25] See Margaret McHenry, *The Ulster Theatre in Ireland* (Philadelphia, 1931).

In sketching the characteristics of the Presbyterian way of life we have come close to describing the Protestant culture as a whole, for what was true of Presbyterians was in large measure true also of Anglicans, Methodists, Baptists, and other smaller sects. This convergence, however, only came about gradually with the decline in the privileged position of the Anglican Church, for while it is true that in terms of rank and social position, Anglicans remained something of a race apart, in other respects the course of events during the nineteenth century had levelled barriers previously thought to be impregnable. The abolition of tithes, the ending of the Anglican monopoly of town government, the abandonment of the practice of appointing Anglican clergy to be Justices of the Peace, the validation of Anglican-Presbyterian marriages performed by Presbyterians, and finally, the formal disestablishment of the Church of Ireland in 1869—all these things helped to prepare the way for a united Protestant opposition to the presumed threat from Catholic nationalism implicit in the Home Rule movement. In the last quarter of the nineteenth century, therefore, it became possible to think, not only in terms of a common political stance held by nearly all Protestants, but of a common outlook upon life. To the credit of this northern Protestantism we can certainly ascribe the traditional Puritan virtues of work, thrift, honesty, and sobriety, together with a strong belief in education and a high regard for learning. And we may fairly apply to Protestants as a whole, the comment of a former Moderator of the Presbyterian Church, when he remarked of his community that it bred 'a sturdy, reasonable and independent type of character, just and scrupulous, careless often of forms and even at times of beauty, but reliable and consistent both in religion and in private and public life.' [26]

Unhappily, as we know, that is not the whole story. The native kindliness and common sense of the Ulster Protestant, which are no different from the native kindliness and common sense of the Ulster Catholic, have not prevented the deep wound

---

passim; D. Kennedy, 'The Drama in Ulster' in *The Arts in Ulster*, pp. 52–7; S. Hanna Bell, *The Theatre in Ulster* (Dublin and London, 1972), chaps. 1 and 2.

[26] J. E. Davey, *1840–1940, the Story of a Hundred Years*, p. 86.

of sectarian bigotry from disfiguring the province throughout its modern history. This, the main cultural constituent of the political anarchy which now besets Northern Ireland, is at once so complex and so esoteric that the outside observer is tempted to recoil from it in baffled disgust. Yet there are two essential keys to the enigma, one belonging to the seventeenth century, one belonging to the nineteenth, and both still relevant at the present day.

The seventeenth-century key derives from those two constants in the Ulster kaleidoscope—land and religion. Because the conquest was gradual, piecemeal, and often precarious, the settlers who struck their roots in the region did so under conditions of maximum insecurity. This insecurity became a permanent part of their psychology. That it should have expressed itself originally in religious terms need not surprise us, when we recall that their physical insecurity was at its most dangerous at the moment when Reformation and Counter-Reformation were locked in combat on a European scale. It was natural for Catholic and Protestant to use the language of damnation in the seventeenth century because both wholeheartedly believed in it. For Catholics, Protestantism represented not merely conquest but also heretical error. For Protestants, Catholicism represented not merely a threat to their economic and social stability but also potential persecution of their inmost beliefs should the balance of power ever change hands again.

Yet while this may be a valid explanation of the seventeenth-century situation, it begs the larger question of why this tension should have persisted unchanged into modern times, when religious conflict was dying out elsewhere. Indeed, it might be asked, did not the eighteenth century indicate that a different pattern of behaviour might have been possible? As we have seen, Presbyterians as well as Catholics had suffered under the penal laws. Influenced by events in America, and later in France, and perhaps predisposed by the democratic structure of their church government, some Presbyterians, mainly of the professional middle class in Belfast (though they also included a number of farmers), developed radical opinions which led them to take a prominent part in the founding of the United Irishmen, the society pledged both to the reconciliation of internal differences and to the ending of English rule. Viewed in retrospect through the haze of romantic nationalism, this has often been seen as the moment when 'Ulster joined Ireland'. This is a profoundly misleading generalization. Some Ulstermen 'joined Ireland', but many more did not. To put the eighteenth century in a true perspective we have to range alongside the Belfast radicals both the Protestant yeomen and the Catholic militiamen who joined in suppressing the United Irishmen.[27]

We have also to find room for the Orange Order. Founded in 1795 after a conflict in county Armagh between Protestant and Catholic societies quarrelling over land, the Orangemen at the outset were pillars of the establishment in church and state. Ostensibly classless, the Order was in fact led by the gentry and stood for the maintenance of the constitution and true (originally Anglican) religion. When insurrection came in 1798 they were an obvious countervailing force, but in fact, as the danger to property grew, and the possibility of a French invasion loomed, most northern Protestants fell in behind the forces of law and order, accepting two years later the abolition of an Irish parliament they had had little cause to love. Yet Presbyterian radicalism, though powerless to overcome the deep divisions in Ulster society, did not disappear with the United Irishmen. On the contrary, right up to the time when Gladstone's adoption of Home Rule forced most, though not all, of them into a unionism which always went somewhat against the grain, Ulster Presbyterians were often not only liberal in politics but also influential in the various movements for the transformation of the tenant-farmers into the owners of their holdings.

There was, however, a limit to this liberalism and before the nineteenth century was two decades old this had begun to emerge. Three developments were significant here. One was that sectarian rivalry, so far from dying out, had begun to spread from the countryside into the larger centres of population. It was ominous

[27] J. C. Beckett, *The Making of Modern Ireland, 1603–1923* (London, 1966), p. 265.

that the first serious riot in Belfast's history, which occurred in 1813, should have been caused by an Orange procession marching through a street mainly inhabited by Catholics. In the next hundred years there were to be fourteen further major outbreaks in Belfast, centring with monotonous regularity on the areas where Catholic and Protestant neighbourhoods coincided and clashed. Not all these were to be laid at the door of the Orange Order which, indeed, was in semi-eclipse for many years. But with the onset of the Home Rule agitation and the closing of ranks between Anglicans and Presbyterians, the Order did become increasingly the focus, not merely of negative anti-Catholic sentiment, but of positive identification with the Protestant myth.

This, as always, was the myth of siege, but it was no less the myth of deliverance from siege. Its history was the history of 1641, 1689, 1690. Its folk-heroes were William of Orange and the Reverend George Walker, the defender of Derry. Its sacred festivals were the commemoration of the Boyne on 12 July and the march of the Apprentice Boys in mid-August to celebrate the raising of the Derry siege. It appealed to religious primitivism, but it also provided colour, poetry, and its own kind of magic for ordinarily drab lives. We can see this in the popular art which Orangeism evoked—in the elaborately decorated banners, with the ever-present William on his white horse, or Queen Victoria presenting bibles to grateful natives, or other figures—even the unlikely Disraeli—added as the exigencies of the time might dictate. We see it again in the triumphal, castellated arches which for many years were erected in key strategic areas—for example, Sandy Row or the Shankill Road—to be guarded like the ark of the covenant from attack by the nearby Catholics of the Falls Road or Divis Street. We see it most strongly in the processions themselves with their Orange flutes and the thundering Lambeg drums which pride demanded should be beaten, or 'chapped' with canes, until the knuckles of the drummers ran with blood.[28] It was here that the dualism of militant Protestantism was most

[28] For a modern account of how 'to chap the Lambeg', see S. Hanna Bell, *Erin's Orange Lily* (London, 1956), chap. 1.

clearly exposed. Here was the visible contrast between the brilliant barbarity of the setting, with its noise and glitter, and the sobriety of the serried ranks of grim and serious and utterly respectable marchers, each in his bowler hat and dark suit crossed by the sash of the lodge of the Order to which he belonged. Here, in formidable juxtaposition, were the immobility and the dynamism of the Protestant culture, the mingling of resolution and hysteria.

The fact that these parades so often led to ferocious clashes with the Catholics is directly related to the two other developments of the nineteenth century which contributed to the deep divisions within the province. The first of these was greatly stimulated by the evangelical awakening by which, as we have already seen, the Protestant churches were so powerfully affected in the mid-nineteenth century. Evangelicalism was accompanied by prosely-tizing zeal which in Belfast often took the form of open-air revivalist meetings whereat perfervid preachers lashed their audiences into fury against Rome and all its works. This preaching not only kept alive the religious dimension of the quarrel in the technical sense, it also, as in 1857, precipitated riot and blood-shed. On that occasion it was an Anglican sermon that was the catalyst for two months of disturbance in which many were injured and much property destroyed. Even this, however, paled into insignificance when Protestant anger at the unveiling of the O'Connell monument in Dublin produced in 1864 eighteen days of riot in Belfast during which twelve people were killed and a hundred injured. And that in turn was a minor affair compared with the Home Rule riots of 1886 in which thirty-two people died. If anything, the disturbances increased in frequency and intensity as time went on. In the first half of the century the detonating event was usually a parliamentary election, but in and after 1857 it was often an Orange, or occasionally a nationalist, procession that provided the *casus belli*.[29]

Such collisions confront us with the last and most important element in this tragic situation, the movement into Belfast (and

[29] Ian Budge and Cornelius O'Leary, *Belfast: Approach to Crisis* (London, 1973), chap. 3, especially the table on p. 89.

into other towns, notably Londonderry) of large numbers of Catholics. By the end of the nineteenth century Catholics accounted for about a quarter of the population of Belfast. These immigrants from the country brought with them certain characteristics derived from their environment and their history. Up to the Great Famine, Ulster, because of its relative isolation, had retained to a greater extent than any other part of Ireland, except the remote west and south-west, primitive agriculture, archaic pastoral practices, the language and folklore of the Gael, the belief in the supernatural, and even the superstitious survival of druidic traditions. This had been made possible by the concentration of extended families—or kinship groups—into settlements known variously as 'clachans', or 'towns', or 'closes', or 'onsets'. This clannishness had begun to break up before the Famine, but that catastrophe, and some subsequent bad seasons, accelerated the process by which the individual farmer struck out on his own, fending for himself and his immediate dependants in remote and lonely homesteads.

While this very loneliness no doubt stimulated the drift to the towns, it had the consequence of making the Ulsterman who stayed on the land a highly self-sufficient person. Districts were so separate from each other that movement in or out of them, except for actual emigration, tended to be minimal. But because in many parts of Ulster, especially in the south and west, the haphazard nature of the conquest and settlement had meant that Catholic and Protestant were not distributed in solid, easily recognizable blocs, and instead were interspersed amongst each other in tiny islands, the necessity to keep one's distance and preserve one's identity was paramount from the beginning. Particularity was so intense that even the most humdrum details of daily life served to mark the difference between Protestant and Catholic. A classic instance is spade cultivation. This was widespread throughout the province, but a man's religious affiliation was immediately deducible from the design of his spade, and whether he put his weight on the right or left of the shaft; 'to dig with the wrong foot' thus became one among many of the signals which the countryman early learned to distinguish.

In socio-economic terms, it is true, there was a more obvious kind of distinction to be made. Broadly speaking, Protestants occupied the lowlands and Catholics the higher, harsher land on the hillsides. The gap between the mountainy people and the lowlanders remained wide and unbridged. No lowlander would contemplate marrying 'up the hill', for that would be a mixed marriage—the unthinkable, unforgivable sin. But it was not only religion, it was a whole way of life which divided these two communities. The hill-people, being poorer, set much store by co-operative labour and among them the habit of visiting, chiefly by the men—'ceilidheing' as it was called—persisted longer than elsewhere. In the lowlands there were sharper gradations of wealth and status. Visiting was much more *en famille* and it was a formal act, nearly as formal as church-going which was a social as well as a religious function. 'The society of the hills is an egalitarian society,' a modern observer has written, 'where everyone is the social and economic equal of everyone else, the society of the lowland farms is a society of social classes. This is a fundamental fact about rural Ulster.'[30]

When Catholic country people moved into Belfast, and to a lesser extent into Derry, to meet the labour demands of rapidly developing industrialism, they were ill-equipped for the transition and gravitated to the bottom of the economic and social scale, being concentrated for the most part in the poorest paid and most menial employment.[31] Again, because of their traditional attachment to the family as a social unit, an attachment much fostered by their Church, they tended to move in groups rather than as individuals and thus to be harder to assimilate. Assimilation would in any case have been difficult because of their previous history. Isolated and on the defensive as we have seen them to be, they had reacted to their predicament by forming their own secret agrarian societies which carried on a running vendetta with similar societies on the Protestant side. Coming from such a

[30] J. M. Mogey, 'Social Relations in Rural Society' in T. W. Moody and J. C. Beckett (ed.), *Ulster ince 1800* (second series, London, 1957), p. 76. See also the same author's *Rural Life in Northern Ireland* (London, 1947), *passim*.
[31] Emrys Jones, *A Social Geography of Belfast* (London, 1960), chap. 13.

background, it was natural that they should congregate from the beginning in particular streets and neighbourhoods. Poor Protestants arriving from a similar environment did much the same, but since Catholic families tended to be larger, and since their employment was generally lower-grade, and since they were in a numerical minority, they adopted more readily a ghetto mentality.

Their isolation was intensified by the ideas and beliefs they brought with them. They were suspect not only because they were Catholics, but because, since O'Connell, they were identified with the agitation to repeal the Union and were thus, by definition, 'disloyal'. Worse still, when it became clear that nationalism could mean not just constitutional pressure for limited self-government, but actual rebellion for total independence, it was easy for Protestants to ignore the real shades of difference among Catholics and to think of them collectively as 'Fenians'. And if this were not enough, the Gaelic revival introduced yet another divisive factor. Not all Ulster Protestants were against the resurgence of the old Irish culture—far from it.[32] And not all Ulster Catholics cared to support that resurgence. Nevertheless, it would be broadly true to say that the ideals of the Gaelic League appealed more strongly to the Catholic than to the Protestant community—naturally, since the League sought to restore the civilization which had been shattered by the Plantations.

These cultural differences need to be stressed because they bear directly upon one interpretation of the communal frictions in Belfast which is often made nowadays—that the religious labels merely concealed a conflict of economic interests, in crude terms that the root of the trouble was competition for jobs, competition artfully encouraged by employers who thus avoided the danger of having to confront a united labour movement. No doubt at

[32] An outstanding example was Bulmer Hobson, of Protestant stock from county Tyrone and a member of the Society of Friends until he withdrew from it in 1914 as being inconsistent with his membership of the Irish Volunteers. One of the pioneers of the Gaelic League in Belfast (where he was much influenced by Alice Milligan) Hobson was also one of the founders of the Ulster Literary Theatre. See his *Ireland Yesterday and Tomorrow* (Tralee, 1968), chaps. 1 and 2.

some periods some employers may have acted deliberately in this way, but it would be unwise to attempt to explain the whole complex quarrel in such simple terms. We have seen, for example, that sectarian rioting began in 1813, long before Catholics were numerous enough to constitute a threat to employment, when in fact they were needed for certain kinds of labour. We know also that most of the collisions before 1857 arose out of elections. And even in 1857, though that was a depression year, the worst unemployment came after the riots were over. In 1864, a year of exceptionally severe fighting, the city was enjoying boom conditions, and although 1886 was a bad year for trade, the shipyards and docks, the centres of disturbance, were in full employment.[33] This is not to say that anxiety among Protestants about competition from cheaper Catholic labour did not exist, and it is virtually certain that as the Ulster economy became more vulnerable in the twentieth century, that anxiety increased. Economic friction has without question been one factor in fomenting bitterness, but there were others, two of which have yet to be mentioned.

The first of these was education. When in 1831 a national system of education was established, the intention was to assist primary education by making state grants available for the building, repair, and equipment of schools, and in aid of teachers' salaries. There was to be no interference with the religious beliefs of children, and religious instruction was to be given to children in their own segregated denominations at times set apart for the purpose. This was about equally offensive to all the Churches, but it was the Presbyterians who made the first major breach in the system in 1840, by forcing a revision of the rules enabling them to refuse to admit ministers of other religions into their schools. Neither did they accept any obligation to ensure that children of other denominations should leave their classroom while Presbyterian religious instruction was being given. Not surprisingly, other denominations shunned mixed schooling conceived on that basis. Two important results followed. One was a grotesque multiplication of small primary schools, reflecting the

[33] Ian Budge and Cornelius O'Leary, *Belfast: Approach to Crisis*, pp. 91–5.

fragmentation of Ulster Protestantism. The other was that the Catholic Church remained firmly outside the state system, a voluntary exclusion which continued after Northern Ireland had come into being. There was the more reason for them to maintain this attitude in that after 1920 Protestant pressure on the Northern Ireland government was strenuously exerted to ensure that state educational segregation was preserved and that Protestant schools should receive more favourable treatment in the expenditure of public funds. Finance apart, however, it has to be said that the objective of segregation was eagerly sought by Catholics as well as Protestants. As a modern authority has commented: 'Despite their detestation of each other, the educational principles of Protestant and Catholic clergymen have been remarkably similar on pivotal issues . . . one finds that the religious leaders of both groups believed that Ulster's children should be taught by teachers of their own denomination, that children should attend school with their co-religionists, and that religious instruction should be woven into the school curriculum.'[34] Such segregated education has been an important part of the cultural divide since early in the nineteenth century. And it has achieved and maintained this central importance because the Churches have always taken it for granted that to control the religious education of their children was essential to survival.[35]

The other development which helped to sharpen antagonisms during the nineteenth and early twentieth centuries was what might be described as the nationalization of Irish politics. Improved communications between Dublin and the north and the evolution of a modern electoral system brought the northern province increasingly into the main stream of events. This had two quite different effects upon Ulster attitudes. On the one hand, where a community of interest obviously existed—as in the land question, for example, or in the periodic agitation against the over-taxation of Ireland—then Ulster was not only indis-

---

[34] Donald H. Akenson, *Education and Enmity: the Control of Schooling in Northern Ireland, 1920–50* (Newton Abbot, 1973), p. 194.

[35] The nineteenth-century background is in Donald H. Akenson, *The Irish Education Experiment* (London, 1970).

tinguishable from the rest of Ireland but was capable of taking a leading part. On the other hand, as nationalist aspirations became more sharply defined, so also did an Ulster sense of difference. The logical end of the Home Rule movement, after all, was the creation of a self-governing Ireland in which Protestants would be in a permanent and decisive minority. Once this realization had sunk in, and once it became clear that the main burden of resistance would fall on the northern Protestants, a *sauve qui peut* mentality almost inevitably developed. The stages by which Irish Unionist opposition to Home Rule became effectively Ulster Unionist opposition need not concern us—what is important is to note that there emerged from this process a form of Ulster separatism which produced the partition settlement of 1920–1.

The obverse of this coin was that Ulster Catholics, seeing their local situation as part of a much larger Irish situation, became more intransigent while looking with increasing urgency for help from their co-religionists in the rest of Ireland. They were encouraged in this attitude by the relative success of the Home Rule party in repeated elections in the last quarter of the nineteenth century and the first decade of the twentieth. In the crucial campaign of 1885, for example, nationalists won a bare majority (seventeen seats to sixteen) in the nine counties of historic Ulster, and although this proved to be exceptional the two sides were so evenly balanced that it was possible for each to discount the overweening claims of the other. But the sense of belonging to the rest of Ireland was greatly enhanced for the Catholics by the formation in the 1880s of their counterpart to the Orange Order. This was the Board of Erin wing of the Ancient Order of Hibernians, a society originating amongst Irish-Americans intent upon demonstrating their Irishness. Its guiding genius in the early years of the new century was the Belfast Catholic, Joseph Devlin, who became also the chief political organizer of the Home Rule party, thus identifying still further the cause of Ulster nationalism with that of Irish nationalism. But when in the end the Home Rule party failed to prevent partition, and when the Ulster Catholics found themselves enclosed within a six-county state designed to make them a permanent minority, it was in the nature of things that they, too, should develop their variant of the siege mentality.

Nowadays, the Ulster question is often described as a tale of three cities—Belfast, Dublin, and London—but though that is obviously true, it would be still more pertinent to think of it primarily as a tale of two minorities—the actual Catholic minority within the present Northern Ireland and the potential Protestant minority which would become actual were Ireland ever to be united. In this lecture we have seen something of the complexity in which Ulstermen, indeed Irishmen, of all creeds and allegiances are caught up when they consider the seemingly insoluble problem which the north presents. In laying stress upon the conflict of cultures there, and especially upon the dominance of the Presbyterian ethos, I have tried to indicate the historic roots of difference in the province. The ancient quarrel is, of course, about power, and about its economic base as well as about its political manifestations. But such clichés can hardly satisfy us. If we ask further what are the ends for which the possession of power is coveted, we may perhaps come closer to the truth about Ulster.

In that small and beautiful region different cultures have collided because each has a view of life which it deems to be threatened by its opponents and power is the means by which a particular view of life can be maintained against all rivals. These views of life are founded upon religion because this is a region where religion is still considered as a vital determinant of everything important in the human condition. And religion is vital because there have been in conflict three (latterly two) deeply conservative, strongly opinionated communities each of whose Churches still expresses what the members of these Churches believe to be the truth. The northern Protestant who exhibits each year afresh his siege mentality when he celebrates Derry and the Boyne is, from his standpoint, right to do so, because this marks not only his thanks for past relief, but also his continuing determination not to allow his hard-won individuality to be submerged in an all-Ireland republic. To dismiss his objections to

Catholic control of education and Catholic attitudes towards such matters as divorce and contraception as factious, because the permissive society is as likely to be repellent to him as to any Roman Catholic bishop, is entirely to miss the point. He resents the intrusion in these matters of any Church save his own, because the history of his Church, by and large, is a history in which laymen have long participated in deciding major issues of policy and in which they have generally resisted the imposition of ecclesiastical authority. The spectre of 1641 is not the spectre of imagined massacre, it is the spectre of a real apprehension of the invasion of private judgement by external forces. Yet the Catholic equally, from his standpoint, cannot come to terms with a culture which despises his faith as obscurantist, but which he himself can only regard as the fruit of conquest and of heresy. Against the Protestant fear of discrimination in the future, he opposes the Catholic experience of discrimination in the past.

That both sides should constantly appeal to history and should continue to use a sectarian terminology which the world has long discarded, constantly baffles outside observers. Yet it should not do so. The history and the terminology are unavoidable because they relate to unfinished business. They are alive today—and this is pre-eminently the sense in which the seventeenth century lives on in Ulster—because the sequence of events over more than three hundred years has ensured that the issues raised when the different cultures first mingled on that 'narrow ground' should still be crucial issues. The context changes but the issues remain identical. That is why the Ulster situation can only be understood, however dimly, in its historical context. To seek to lay bare the historical roots of difference will not necessarily lead us to a solution. But the recognition of difference, especially by Irishmen themselves, is a prerequisite for peaceful coexistence. Such recognition, if it did nothing else, might at least bring us one stage further towards that sympathetic insight which is what the problem has always demanded but too seldom received.

6

At Opposite Poles

It is difficult, after a lapse of more than half a century, to capture the mood of mingled hope and bitterness with which in 1922 the Irish Free State began its career as an independent nation. The hope sprang naturally from the establishment of an Irish government on Irish soil for the first time for seven hundred years. The bitterness, of course, was partly due to the fact that independence began in the midst of civil war, for although that struggle ended in 1923 with the defeat of the republicans, it left a legacy of instability and hatred which were to poison Irish life for two generations. But partly also men were bitter because it was not the nation of their dreams which the settlement of 1921 had brought to birth. At last they had had to confront the realization that the ideal of a united Ireland, even if not abandoned, had seemingly to be laid aside for an indefinite future.

Perhaps the most important consequence of the incompleteness of the 1921 settlement was that by concentrating attention on physical boundaries and questions of political sovereignty, it postponed almost until our own day any serious consideration of the cultural differences that underlay the partition of the country. Indeed, so far were the new rulers of the Irish Free State from recognizing the existence of these cultural differences, that they immediately proceeded to implement a series of policies which, however logical in the context of the twenty-six counties of the Free State, were liable to evoke—and did evoke—hostility and suspicion in the six counties of Northern Ireland.

To say that these policies were logical in the context of the twenty-six counties is to say that they were both Gaelic and Catholic. They were also both innovatory and conservative. The policy of Gaelicization was indeed both innovatory and conservative at the same time. It was designed to save a language which appeared to be dying, but in order to save it, there had to be a revolutionary break with the past. By 1922 it was painfully obvious that Irish, as a sole language, was the possession of a tiny minority of people, and that even as a working language in a bilingual context it was being used by fewer and fewer. To retrieve this situation two things were held to be paramount. First, everything possible had to be done to preserve the Gaeltacht, which was seen as the well of Irish pure and undefiled from whose clear but diminishing waters the rest of the country might be succoured. Secondly, so that the rest of the country should be able to derive full benefit from the Gaeltacht, the Irish language had to be implanted at the heart of the educational system, even to the extent of having other subjects taught through that medium. Within weeks of coming into office the Provisional Government of 1922 ordained that Irish should be taught or used as a medium of instruction for not less than an hour a day in all primary schools where there was a properly qualified teacher. By 1926, despite intensive cramming, only about half the primary school teachers could meet the government requirements though thereafter the situation steadily improved. Ironically, however, the Irish National Teachers' Organisation, after some years' experience of teaching 'through the medium', came out strongly against this practice on general educational grounds, and from about 1950 onwards it seems to have been progressively relaxed. In the secondary schools, where Irish was already fairly well established before independence, it was made a compulsory subject for the Intermediate and Leaving Certificates, while at the same time its use and teaching were encouraged by financial rewards both to schools and to individual teachers.[1]

---

[1] *An Coimisiún um Athbheochan na Gaelige* (Commission on the restoration of the Irish language), summary, in English, of the final report, 1963 (Pr. 7256), pp. 11–12. More recent figures, indicating a continuous decline, are in Tomás Ó Domhnalláin, 'An Gaeilge san Oideachas–Fás nó Meath', in *Teangeolas*, No. 7 (spring 1978); I owe this reference to Professor Máirtín Ó Murchú of Trinity College, Dublin. For the general background, see F. S. L. Lyons, *Ireland Since the Famine*, pp. 635–45.

How far these measures resulted in cultural enrichment for those to whom they were applied has ever since been a subject of acrimonious debate, but at least it cannot be denied that school children of all ages were exposed to their native language with a thoroughness that had not previously been attempted since that language had first begun to go into decline. The second object of policy, however, the preservation of the Gaeltacht, fell so far short of achievement that experts have continued to prophesy that it will be virtually extinct by the end of the century. This approaching extinction is often blamed on the inadequacy and inconsistency of the efforts made by successive governments, but a more potent cause of decay is probably the inexorable pressure of other forces. The chief of these are economic weakness and susceptibility to alien cultural influences. The western and south-western seaboards were among the poorest regions in the country and for that reason particularly open to the lure of emigration which generally took away the younger and more dynamic inhabitants. As a modern authority has written: 'There are whole parishes in Waterford, Cork, Kerry, Clare, Galway, Mayo and Donegal where Irish was the ordinary language at the beginning of the present century in which there now survive only a few aged native speakers.'[2] Where there had been 200,000 estimated Irish speakers in the Gaeltacht in 1922, that number had been halved by 1939, and was to be halved again in the succeeding twenty-five years. Moreover, because these districts are among the most beautiful in Ireland, they are among the most frequented by tourists, so that bilingualism, with an increasing emphasis upon English, has become unavoidable. This, according to some authorities, has led to a decline in the quality of the Irish now used in the Gaeltacht, so that the present generation, it is said, do not speak with the same fluency, precision, or raciness as their monoglot grandparents. And as the old people die out, so too do the storytellers; with them has all but vanished a reservoir of folklore as well as of language.[3]

[2] Caoimhín Ó Danachair, 'The Gaeltacht', in B. Ó Cuív (ed.), *A View of the Irish Language* (Dublin, 1969), p. 119.

[3] Ibid., pp. 119–21.

The desperate and seemingly forlorn attempt to restore the Irish language to the centre of Irish culture was paralleled by a second development which not only met with greater success, but did much to give the new state its distinctive character. This was the strong emphasis that was placed on Catholic teaching, as it impinged on both public and private life. There was nothing new, of course, about the deep devotion of most Irish people to the religion that had sustained them for so many centuries, and we have already seen that even before 1914 there had been something of a religious revival. What happened after 1922 was that with a sympathetic government in power, Catholic doctrines and attitudes, especially on social questions, were much more in harmony with official policy than under British rule, and were therefore more easily translated into acts of policy or, on occasion, into legislation.

There was, admittedly, a danger that the Church, faced for the first time by an Irish administration, might view that administration with the same suspicion it had shown towards the potentially competing power of the Parnellite party forty years earlier. If such suspicion of lay politicians did exist in some clerical quarters, it was kept, on the whole, under tight control, and in the crisis of the civil war the Church threw its weight unreservedly behind the newly established government. In doing so it helped, whether consciously or not, to strengthen the secular arm, not merely because it upheld the status quo, but because, by committing itself so wholeheartedly to one side on an issue which had divided men so deeply, it could be held to have threatened its own power-base in the country as a whole. As one of the losers in the civil war put it, the hierarchy, having thrown bell, book and candle at the republic, 'drove one half of the people against them with the result that they never regained the power they once had'.[4] This may be something of an exaggeration. No doubt the Church's excommunication of militant republicans caused lasting resentment among those so singled out, but it is probably fair to say that most republicans in the 1920s, like most Fenians in the 1860s, distinguished in their own minds and to their own satisfaction

[4] Patrick O'Farrell, *Ireland's English Question*, pp. 296–7.

between spiritual matters, in which they willingly acknowledged ecclesiastical authority, and public life, where laymen had to exercise their private judgement. This delicate balance could only be maintained so long as the boundary·between the spiritual and the political was not defined too precisely, but the Church itself was unlikely to demand that it should be. There was a long tradition whereby, under British rule, the Church had deliberately held aloof from the state and the fact that the state was now 'native' did not imply any necessity for change. It is true that in the constitution of 1937 Mr de Valera inserted a clause recognizing the 'special position' of the Catholic Church, but it is doubtful if that could ever have had a juridical status, and it seems to have had little or no effect in practice.[5]

Not too much, however, should be made of the formal separation of the civil and the ecclesiastical powers, for in the things that really mattered there was no serious disagreement between the bishops and the secular rulers of the country. Education, for example, always a prime concern of the Church, remained at all levels firmly in a Catholic context, and in other spheres successive governments either initiated proposals themselves, or responded to suggestions from others in such a way as to strengthen the Catholic element in Irish culture. In 1923, for example, the Censorship of Films Act established a film censor with powers to 'cut' films, or refuse them a licence altogether if he found them 'subversive of public morality', which meant, in effect, Catholic morality. In 1925 the government carried a motion in the Dáil which made it impossible for private divorce bills to be introduced there, and the head of the government, Mr W. T. Cosgrave, publicly announced his support for the sanctity of the marriage bond; divorce, in the full sense of dissolution of the marriage tie with freedom to remarry, remained impossible under Irish law. In 1929 came the Censorship of Publications Act which did two things. First, it set up a Censorship Board of five persons (originally one Protestant and three Catholic laymen with a Catholic priest as chairman) with power to prohibit the sale and distribution of any book or periodical which

[5] The clause was repealed by referendum in 1972.

it considered 'in its general tendency indecent or obscene'; in its notorious exercise of this power over the years the Board banned some or all of the work of most of the major European, American, and Irish writers. Secondly, the act made the publication, sale, or distribution of literature advocating birth-control an offence.[6]

There was no deviation from this readiness of the state to underwrite Catholic morality when Mr Cosgrave's government gave way in 1932 to that of Mr de Valera. Mr de Valera's party, Fianna Fáil, seemed, indeed, even more ready to equate 'Irish' with 'Catholic' than their predecessors, and Mr de Valera on more than one occasion used language which indicated that he thought of Ireland primarily as a Catholic nation.[7] In terms of legislation, he simply continued where Mr Cosgrave had left off. Thus in 1933 the budget included a tax on imported newspapers, something which would-be censors had been demanding since the foundation of the State. In 1935 the law regarding contraceptives was amended so as to make their sale and importation a criminal offence. And in that year also the government stepped in to do by statute what the bishops had failed to do by exhortation, requiring public dance-halls—which to the clerical imagination were nurseries of every sort of vice—to obtain a licence from the magistrate for each dance held therein.

The climax of this tendency to embody Catholic teaching in the law of the land was reached in the constitution of 1937. Not only did this include the clause already referred to which distinguished the 'special position' of the Catholic Church, but the clauses relating to the family, to marriage, to education, and even to property, all reflected Catholic social teaching. This in turn reflected a growing awareness of the movement of Catholic thought on the continent. Such awareness had been strikingly absent from nineteenth-century Ireland. At that time isolation from Europe had been largely unavoidable, partly because clerical energies had been fully engaged in building churches, in creating a Catholic school system and, to some extent at least, in

[6] Michael Adams, *Censorship: the Irish Experience* (Dublin, 1968), chaps. 2 and 3.
[7] J. H. Whyte, *Church and State in Modern Ireland, 1923–1970* (Dublin and London, 1971), p. 48.

supplying leadership in the various political and agrarian agitations. But partly also this isolation was due to the virtual non-existence of a Catholic intelligentsia. 'Among the Catholics of Ireland,' wrote a shrewd French observer in 1907, 'even among the liberal classes, there are but few to be found who possess any real culture. We find, on the contrary, a certain form of intellectual apathy very widespread, a distaste for mental effort, a certain absence of the critical sense.'[8] Some of this backwardness probably derived from a sense of inferiority which, among those who essayed to climb the social ladder, expressed itself in an unconvincing attempt to ape the manners and intellectual style of educated Protestants. But it was still more a consequence of the late arrival of an effective Catholic university. This deficiency began to be remedied when the Jesuits took over Newman's university in 1883, but it was only with the creation of the National University in 1908 that Catholic Ireland got the university it needed and craved. Within a generation the graduates of the new university had begun to make a substantial contribution to both the public and the intellectual life of the country.

The first evidence of the emergence of a more informed Catholicism dated from the very year of the Anglo-Irish treaty. In October 1921, arising out of a conference held by the Society of St Vincent de Paul, a layman and a priest together founded the Legion of Mary, designed, as its handbook stated, to be at the disposal of the clergy 'for any and every form of social service and Catholic action which the authorities may deem suitable to the Legionaries and useful for the welfare of the Church'. Gradually this spread all over Ireland and then throughout the world. From the start it was distinguished from the ordinary run of charitable organizations by avoiding material assistance and concentrating—for example, in prayer meetings and house-to-house visits—on what its literature described as 'the permeation of the community with Catholic principles and Catholic feeling'.[9] The Legion of

---

[8] L. Paul-Dubois, *Contemporary Ireland* (London, 1908: original French edn., Paris, 1907), p. 496.

[9] D. Fennell, *The Changing Face of Catholic Ireland* (London, 1968), pp. 65, 67.

Mary was followed a few years later by another organization, An Rioghacht (The Kingdom), which was a federation of study circles specializing in the discussion of Catholic social principles. Such discussion was greatly stimulated by the publication in 1931 of Pope Pius XI's encyclical, *Quadragesimo Anno*, an attempt to restate in contemporary terms the doctrine enshrined in *Rerum Novarum* forty years previously. The intention of both encyclicals was to promote social harmony between classes by advocating that industries and professions should be organized in vocational 'groups' or 'corporations' in which workers and employers were intended to co-operate, thus relegating the state to a supervisory role. In Ireland, where Mussolini's version of the corporative state had made some notable converts, *Quadragesimo Anno* seemed to offer an alternative to economic anarchy, perhaps even to a descent into totalitarianism in one form or other. Several new initiatives were directly traceable to its influence. One such, Muintir na Tire (People of the Land), bent its efforts, with considerable success, towards humanizing life on the land and making it economically worth while. Another, the Guilds of Regnum Christi, attempted a revival of vocational organization through a guild system. Yet another was the reshaping of *The Standard*, an influential Catholic newspaper, to turn it into a vehicle for corporatist thinking. And more important than any of these was the commitment of several members of the hierarchy, most notably Archbishop John Charles McQuaid of Dublin, to the improvement of social conditions and the ventilation among Catholics of questions of social welfare.

There was, however, another side to the problem. The concern of the Church was not merely with doctrine and law, but also with social behaviour, behaviour which continued to be affected long after independence, not merely by the unsettlement of the war years, but also by the continuing threat to Catholic purity and innocence of foreign—more specifically, English—influences. At one level this concern took the form of crude and hectoring propaganda, as purveyed, for instance, by magazines such as *Catholic Mind* or the *Catholic Bulletin* which, when they were not excoriating Trinity College or the remnants of the ascendancy, were either attacking each other or demanding an ever more stringent enforcement of Catholic morality.[10] But at a more sophisticated and more effective level, moral policing was demanded also by the hierarchy, obsessed by the way in which occasions of sin seemed to be steadily multiplying, especially in those pernicious dance-halls. 'The old Irish dances', one archbishop remarked in 1926, 'had been discarded for foreign importations which, according to all accounts, lent themselves not so much to rhythm as to low sensuality ... Company-keeping under the stars of night had succeeded in too many places to the good old Irish custom of visiting, chatting and story-telling from one house to another, with the rosary to bring all home in due time.'[11] Nor was the archbishop alone in his anxieties. In 1927 the bishops issued a joint pastoral lamenting the decline in parental authority and discipline. 'The evil one is forever setting his snares for unwary feet. At the moment, his traps for the innocent are chiefly the dance-hall, the bad book, the indecent paper, the motion picture, the immodest fashion in female dress—all of which tend to destroy the characteristic virtues of our race.'[12] The clergy, it must be said, were not backward in their efforts to stop the rot. In parish after parish they broke up the open-air dancing platforms, destroyed the ubiquitous concertinas, haunted the country lanes to the terror of courting couples, while one priest even achieved a kind of immortality by insisting that in the local cinema men should sit on one side of the aisle and women on the other.

That clergymen should take a puritanical attitude towards sex was perhaps understandable in the light of their own commitment to chastity, but this does not explain either why they should have been able to impose their ideas so easily upon their flocks, or why, as was apparently the case, their preoccupation with sexual dangers should have become more intense during the first generation of Irish independence. It is certainly no answer to attribute these phenomena, as has sometimes been done, to some

---

[10] Michael Adams, *Censorship: the Irish Experience*, pp. 65–8.
[11] J. H. Whyte, *Church and State in Modern Ireland, 1923–1970*, p. 25.
[12] Ibid., p. 27.

vague 'inherent characteristic' of Irish society, or to some putative injection of Jansenism into the priesthood from the early days of Maynooth when its first professors had come from the continent. Nor is it enough to link this puritanical view of life with the desire, common enough in the wake of a successful revolution, to demonstrate that the new world was not only free but also purged of the vices of the old. We know, on the contrary, that observers had been commenting on the joylessness of the Irish countryside at least since the early days of the twentieth century.[13]

To explain the acquiescence of the rural population (the slum-dwellers of the tenements of the larger towns were, of course, in a different situation) in what often amounted to a sexual censor-ship exercised by their priests, we have to look more closely at local patterns of behaviour, but at the same time to guard against the assumption that these were unique. There was, after all, a widespread belief in western Europe that conventional morality had declined in the post-war decades and one can easily find evidence of alarm in many countries about, for example, the traffic in obscene literature or the supposed evils that blossomed in unregulated dance-halls. But if in Ireland we are dealing with a regional variation upon an international theme, we have to recognize that that variation was shaped by history. More particularly, it was shaped in a predominantly rural society by the pressures of population upon a limited supply of land. It is true that the population was halved in the second part of the nine-teenth century by the Famine and the subsequent emigration, but the memory of that catastrophic time had entered so deeply into the folk-memory of the Irish peasant that his attitudes towards the land were profoundly and permanently affected.

The evil to be avoided at all costs was subdivision of the family farm. The aim to be achieved at all costs was to add to the family farm. The family thus was not merely a social unit, it was also an economic unit, essential to the working of the farm, to its extension and to its preservation from generation to generation.

[13] For example, Sir Horace Plunkett, *Ireland in the New Century*, p. 116; Filson Young, *Ireland at the Cross Roads* (London, 1903), pp. 76–7; W. P. Ryan, *The Pope's Green Island* (London, 1912), p. 79.

The normal sequence was for the farmer to pass on his farm first to his wife and then to one of his sons. This meant not only that the favoured son had usually to delay marriage until the death of both his parents allowed him to enter into his inheritance, but that the other sons, and often enough the daughters as well, were condemned either to emigration or to chastity. For daughters, especially, premarital virginity was not only a moral but also a social imperative, since their marriageability was an important element in the tortuous but life-long endeavour to add field to field. To destroy a girl's 'character' by intercourse outside wedlock was regarded in peasant eyes as 'murder' and actually so called in some parts of the country.[14] All these factors working together helped to produce two outstanding characteristics of Irish peasant society which have been constant from the latter part of the nineteenth century until almost the present day—the high average age of marriage and the large number of elderly un-married people of both sexes. A leading authority on Irish demographic history, Professor Connell, has contended in effect that the task of the clergy was to justify the ways of man to man by enforcing the most rigid sexual discipline upon a population of whom a significant proportion could never hope to marry at all.[15] His findings have been questioned, but there can be little doubt that in a situation where marriage was late and relatively seldom, the Church had somehow to preserve or to assist what in effect amounted to perpetual celibacy for many men and women.

For the young people who had no prospect either of inheritance or of marriage to turn their backs on a society which demanded from them a lifetime of abnegation was a natural reaction. Sometimes, also, there were financial as well as social inducements to leave. One of the hardest lessons that the new generation of Irishmen had to learn was that political independence did not automatically carry with it economic independence. On the

[14] C. M. Arensberg and S. T. Kimball, *Family and Community in Ireland* (Cambridge, Mass., 1968), p. 209.

[15] K. H. Connell, *Irish Peasant Society* (Oxford, 1968), chap. 4, 'Catholicism and Marriage in the Century After the Famine'.

contrary, the Irish Free State remained in all essentials a part of
the economy of the British Isles and a backward part at that, for
which emigration represented both a human tragedy and a hard
necessity. The cultural implications of this outward movement of
population, and of the dependence upon England which it
implied, were profound, but they can be summed up simply
enough. Since, from 1922 onwards, with the virtual closing down
of the American route, Irish emigration was overwhelmingly
directed towards England, the pull of English society, of the
English economy, of English habits and standards, became if
anything even heavier after independence than before it. Most
parts of the country experienced this attraction to greater or lesser
degree, but the west and south-west, already much depopulated
in the nineteenth century, felt it particularly strongly. Thus, not
only were the Irish-speaking regions further denuded of their
people, but, by an almost too cruel irony, many of those who
remained in those emptying vastnesses often were able to do so
only because of the remittances they received from sons and
daughters in England.[16]

When we add to this the coming and going of the emigrants at
holiday time, the continued flow of English newspapers and books
despite the censorship, and the influence of the radio and the
cinema, it is clear that the advancing tide of modernity was
almost irresistible. Of these various alien forces the cinema was
perhaps the most important, spreading as it did from the large
cities into the smallest country towns. To the eyes of anxious
moralists it was in some ways worse than the dreaded dance-halls.
Not only did it add darkness to propinquity, but it held the
mirror up to a way of life very different from that which Catholic
boys and girls had been taught to regard as necessary and right.
With the coming of the talkies the threat was, so to speak,
amplified. 'Sic transit Gloria Swanson', wrote one Irish critic,
mourning the chaste heroines of the silent screen. But much else
passed away also when traditional speech and music and manners
were subjected to the immense pressures generated by Hollywood
in the 1930s. Given the Irish obsession with the evils of modern

[16] F. S. L. Lyons, *Ireland Since the Famine*, pp. 609, 622–3.

dance-music, there was a certain irony in the fact that the first commercial film to use sound successfully should have been *The Jazz-Singer*, typifying nearly everything that Gaelic Ireland did not want to be. And although the cinema paid its belated tribute to that Gaelic Ireland in 1934 with Robert Flaherty's *Man of Aran*, it was impossible not to feel even at the time that at heart this was no more than a magnificent threnody for a dying culture.

It is not surprising that the reaction against this onrush of modernity should have been bitter, more bitter than it had been before 1914 because now the contrast between political independence and cultural mongrelism was harder to bear. Yet the curious thing is that what began as a protest against the enemy without ended by becoming the final round of the old conflict between Irish Ireland and Anglo-Irish Ireland. The sense of *déjà vu* which is almost second nature for every Irish historian is heightened in this instance by the reappearance of the same themes, indeed the same names, as if all had remained unchanged in the interval. Thus D. P. Moran, resuming business in 1919 with his *New Leader*, had clearly learnt nothing and forgotten nothing since 1900. 'With language and industry developing with the active principle of life within them,' he proclaimed, 'the fundamentals of the historic Irish nation are secure; without them the Irish nation is dying.'[17] And although he did not resurrect the old cliché of the battle between two civilizations, others did. One of the young writers to emerge from the revolutionary generation, Eimar O'Duffy, produced in 1919 a bitter novel of disenchantment based on the Easter Rising, *The Wasted Island*. In the course of it a militant patriot attacks a Catholic friend who has grown up in an anglicized environment, living in Ireland but apparently unaware that his country might be in some way different from England:

You know little and care less for her traditions; you don't observe her customs; you don't think as she does; your heroes are not her heroes and your flag is not her flag; and instead of that patriotism which is a natural feeling innate in every normal man you have a bastard thing you call 'loyalty' . . . which is nothing more in reality than the fealty which a garrison owes its paymasters . . .

[17] *The New Leader*, 15 Nov. 1919.

It's a question of life and death with us; a war between two civilisations, with our national language and customs, our very name and existence at stake; and so long as the struggle goes on, nothing else in the world matters to us.[18]

The descent from that kind of rhetoric to what Yeats once called 'this pragmatical, preposterous pig of a world' is generally painful and so the advocates of thorough-going Gaelicization found it. Although the state, as we have seen, was fully committed to compulsory Irish in the schools, and although there was certainly a public opinion in favour of that policy, there was always an undercurrent of doubt about its wisdom, even among some whose affection for the language was unquestioned. Take, for example, the clash that occurred in 1924 between that most militant of republicans, Mary MacSwiney, and Sean O'Casey, then in the first flush of his fame as a dramatist. Miss MacSwiney thought the official policy half-hearted. 'While an Irish government,' she wrote, 'will not allow English to be caned out of Irish children as it was caned into them, the outcry against compulsory Irish is as hypocritical as it is unnatural . . .' She later amended this to remove the impression that she was in fact in favour of caning English out of school-children, but she remained adamant for rigorous compulsion.[19] O'Casey disagreed with her vehemently. Himself a fluent Irish speaker, he was totally opposed to forcing the language upon half-starved children from the tenements he knew so well. The whole business, he said, was 'a fancy fraud and a gigantic sham'. Of thirty-four advertisements in a recent issue of a leading Irish-language magazine, only three had been in Irish, he pointed out. And he added: 'Let us take the question of culture pure and simple. What is the teaching of Irish in the schools going to do for culture: what can it do? In this matter, culture can come to the children only through the teachers; and they, forlorn enough as they are in English, a language which they know, how can they excel in Irish, a language which they don't know?'[20]

[18] Eimar O'Duffy, *The Wasted Island* (London, 1929, revised edn. of work first published in 1919), pp. 113–14.

[19] *The Leader*, 6 and 24 Dec. 1924. Moran's paper had resumed its old title on 12 June 1920.

[20] *Irish Statesman*, 19 Jan. 1925.

The argument about compulsion was to rage for decades to come, but without any noticeable effect upon government thinking, which remained firmly committed to 'essential Irish' throughout the period covered by these lectures. But there were those who feared for the outcome, especially in the absence of suitable texts for schools and colleges. To impose Irish on the schools without such texts, or without adequately trained teachers, would, thought one observer sympathetic to the revival, be suicidal, producing either hatred of the language, or illiteracy, or both. For him, as for others, the key lay in preserving the Gaeltacht where Irish was the normal language of communication.[21] But was this really so? O'Casey, for one, doubted it. The mode of thought of a midland peasant, he suggested, was fundamentally different from that of a Gaeltacht resident, and it was unfair to impose on the former what belonged to the latter. 'Briefly, the mentality and tradition of the children of the Gaeltacht to-day is, let us say, "Irish". Outside the Gaeltacht it is "English" if you will.'[22] O'Casey himself, of course, opted for English with his own characteristic Dublin inflection, but others continued to be plagued with doubts about the resources available, pointing out the dearth of Irish books in every branch of learning at both secondary school and university level. As Sean O'Faoláin, one of a handful of creative writers in Irish and English, remarked in 1925, what was really needed was humanistic scholarship. Had the universities grappled with that task, he said, 'we should not now be left with one or two novels, not a single serious drama, and not a solitary work of literary criticism'.[23]

The situation, admittedly, improved slightly during the next decade and three autobiographical works, Tomás Ó Criomhthain's *An tOileánach* (*The Islandman*), Peig Sayers's *Peig* and Muiris Ó Súilleabháin's *Fiche Bliadhan ag Fás* (*Twenty Years a-Growing*), each achieved wide fame when translated into

[21] L. Garret, 'The Gaelicisation of Irish Education', I, in *Irish Statesman*, 24 May 1924.

[22] *Irish Statesman*, 5 July 1924.

[23] *Irish Statesman*, 14 Nov. 1925. See also Donal McCartney, 'A Nationalist Right Enough', in *Irish University Review*, vol. vi, no. 1, spring 1976 (an issue celebrating Seán O'Faoláin's seventy-fifth birthday), pp. 73–86.

English and other languages. But they were all concerned with
life in West Kerry or off the Kerry coast, and they were essentially
vehicles for nostalgia rather than harbingers of a modern literature.
Modernity, so far as it existed at all, was represented by a few
urban writers of fiction, a handful of poets, and one serious
historian, Leon Ó Broin. The list of authors and of works
remained scanty until the onset of the Second World War, when
the isolation imposed on Ireland by neutrality coincided with the
emergence into adult life of the first generation of those who,
while mostly not native-speakers, had received their full exposure
to Irish at school. The war, which changed so much in Ireland,
was a turning-point also for the movement to develop a modern
literature in the Irish language. Nevertheless, one must not
exaggerate. Even with the various kinds of encouragement to
publication which proliferated after 1945, even with the emergence of notable prose-writers like Máirtín Ó Cadhain, and
notable poets like Máire Mhac an tSaoi and Seán Ó Ríordáin, and
even though after the foundation of An Club Leabhar in 1948 a
book accepted by the club was guaranteed a sale of 3,000 copies,
the number of books actually published remained few enough. So
few, indeed, that it was estimated in 1969 that the total number of
books printed in Irish since the beginning of the century was 'far
less' than a single year's production in England.[24]

The Irish language movement was thus a frail enough barrier
against the increasing encroachment of Anglo-American civilization and, as we saw earlier, the number of Irish speakers continued
steadily to decline. Yet the emphasis on revival, still more the
parallel emphasis upon producing a Catholic nation, proved to be
as divisive, if not more so, after 1919 as before 1914. By the latter
date, it is true, the balance of power had shifted. In Northern
Ireland, where politicians spoke openly of ruling over 'a Protestant people', the preoccupation of the south with Gaelicism and
Catholicism was as repugnant as the constant clamour against
partition which emanated from Dublin with no sign of a constructive idea as to how this might best be achieved. Whatever

[24] Gearóid S. Mac Eoin, 'Twentieth Century Irish Literature', in Brian Ó Cuív
(ed.), *A View of the Irish Language*, pp. 57–69.

common ground had existed between Ulster and the rest of Ireland during the period of the Union was largely lost to view as the two entities found themselves increasingly at opposite poles. In each part of the island there was now a minority, but whereas in the north that minority amounted to a third of the population and was bitterly resentful of what it regarded as the unfair discrimination exercised against it by the majority, in the south the minority only amounted to about five per cent and was, or seemed to be, enervated by the almost repressive tolerance shown to it by the majority.

Yet, in the Irish Free State there were important battles to be fought, battles, as we can now see, which were as relevant to the north as to the south. Because the southern minority was so small and so much on the defensive, these battles tended to be fought out on a narrow front and by a few representative figures. In this final phase of the conflict between the cultures, one journal, the *Irish Statesman*, occupied a key position. Refounded by Sir Horace Plunkett within a few months of the destruction of his Dublin home by republican raiders, it is hardly too much to say that between 1923 and 1930, when lack of resources forced it to close, the *Irish Statesman* was the window through which the less benighted Irishmen sought to look at the world. Virtually every Irish author of note contributed to it, but its high standing was a tribute primarily to the editor, AE, who not only wrote much of the paper himself, but used all his considerable influence to obtain a hearing for the Anglo-Irish viewpoint, and in particular for those who warned against the intellectual and artistic sterility which a too intense concentration upon Gaelicism and Catholicism was liable to induce. AE was not hostile to Irish, not even to compulsory Irish, but he saw it in a bilingual context. That itself was a distant dream, and the foreseeable future, as he recognized, lay with English. But it was still necessary, indeed more than ever necessary, to contend for the artist to be free to express himself as he pleased. It was yet more necessary to insist at all times that Irish history was a history of complexity and that war to the death between the cultures would destroy civilization in every part of the island.

This was the theme he struck in the very first issue of the *Irish Statesman*. It was, he said, to be a national journal, regarding all who lived in the island as one people, whose unity could only be achieved through mutual understanding and friendship. This objective had been obscured by a decade of war and revolution, and now he wanted to bring back to men's minds that fusion of cultures which he, mistakenly, believed had been so nearly achieved in the early years of the century. 'Up to 1914,' he wrote, 'and for nigh a quarter of a century before that, the Irish imagination had begun to work with more intensity on the problem of building up a civilisation with a social order in accordance with national character.' But the struggle for political independence seemed to have swallowed up all other objectives, and herein lay the great danger. 'If we are not to fail to realise our best aspirations we must recall to memory those ideas which made Ireland in the pre-war years so intellectually interesting to ourselves and to other nations.'[25]

That was one way of looking at a situation which AE, habitually optimistic, thought was yet capable of being turned to good account. But there was another more disenchanted way of looking at it, and of this Bernard Shaw was the uncompromising spokesman. The Irish, he argued, were so sunk in their old-fashioned romantic nationalism that it would pass the wit of man to wake them out of it. Nevertheless, he proposed to try:

Now Ireland is at this moment a regular rag and bottle shop of superseded ideas or superstitions . . . There are formidable vested interests in our huge national stock of junk and bilge, glowing with the phosphorescence of romance. Heroes and heroines have risked their lives to force England to drop Ireland like a hot potato. England, after a final paroxysm of doing her worst, has dropped Ireland accordingly. But in doing so she has destroyed the whole stock-in-trade of the heroes and heroines. The heroes and heroines cannot realise it . . . They will die calling for a forlorn hope to storm Dublin Castle. It has surrendered; but even were it demolished as completely as the Bastille they would never notice it . . .

. . . Nationalism must now be added to the refuse pile of superstitions. We are now citizens of the world; and the man who divides the race into elect Irishmen and reprobate foreign devils (especially Englishmen) had better live

[25] AE, 'A Confession of Faith', in *Irish Statesman*, 15 Sept. 1923.

on the Blaskets where he can admire himself without much disturbance. Perhaps, after all, our late troubles were not so purposeless as they seemed. They were probably ordained to prove to us that we are no better than other people; and when Ireland is once forced to accept this stupendous new idea, good-bye to the old patriotism. We must realise that national independence is now impossible.[26]

What AE feared, and what Shaw predicted, seemed to be coming to pass before their eyes. The new nation was turning in on itself, and in its anxiety to establish a cultural as well as a political independence was intent upon the creation of an exclusively Gaelic-Catholic model. And, although illogical, it was also human that the more obviously out of line with contemporary reality this proved to be, the more bitterly and doggedly it was likely to be pursued; and the more it was pursued, the more blinkered and introverted the pursuers were likely to become. Early in 1924 AE was enraged by a classic instance of this very tendency when a politician went out of his way to proclaim publicly the self-evident proposition that neither he nor his fellow-members of the ruling party could be classed as intellectuals. 'How,' asked AE in despair, 'are we to build up a civilisation worthy of our struggles for freedom and our past traditions if Deputies in the new Ireland begin by decrying intellect . . . when we want above everything else respect for intellect, education, culture and the men of special or expert knowledge?'[27] The answer, he still insisted, could not lie in using the Irish language as a dyke behind which every kind of parochialism could shelter. Cosmopolitanism was too vast, too insistent, too much the spirit of the times to be ignored. 'No doubt in a few years,' he wrote at this time, 'we shall be able to listen to Bolshevist music or hear barbaric tom-toms played by expert performers in Africa, or if the promised television is perfected we shall all be gaping in the theatres while the last candidate for the American presidency conducts his whirlwind campaign, not only for the benefit of his own country-men, but for the world . . .' How, he asked, could Cuchulainn

[26] G. B. S[haw], 'On Throwing Out Dirty Water', in *Irish Statesman*, 15 Sept. 1923.
[27] *Irish Statesman*, 12 Jan. 1924.

hope to compete with that? The only possible solution was co-existence:

We believe we want world culture, world ideas, world science; otherwise Ireland would not be a nation but a parish. We believe ourselves that the ideal of an Irish culture relying upon its own resources is impossible; but a culture more vital is possible, indeed certain, by the wedding of the Gaelic culture to world culture.[28]

AE's critics, oppressed by the very power and ubiquity of the cosmopolitanism that assailed Ireland in so many ways, clung stubbornly to their contention that there would be no Gaelic culture either to wed to world culture or to divorce from it, if the Irish language were not saved. 'The lacuna in his [AE's] thought from the Gaelic point of view,' wrote one of these critics, 'is that he does not tell us how this fire of our own is to be preserved if we have no language of our own to protect us from the flood of English speech and thought and outlook and standardization that threatens at every moment to quench our fire.'[29] Nor were the Gaelic revivalists alone in their fear of the encroaching tide. The Ulster novelist, Shan Bullock, an acute observer of his native countryside, expressed the same anxiety, the same distaste for the readiness with which Irishmen, whatever their origins, embraced what came to them from outside—'the hypocritical subservience', as he put it, 'which rejects a tyranny yet serves the tyrant'. Perhaps it was already too late to do anything about it. 'Perhaps, as some believe, it is hopeless to resist the tremendous, vulgarising power of Anglo-American civilisation.'[30]

AE was unrepentant. Agreeing that Gaelic culture was necessary to the continuance of a separate Irish identity, he still insisted upon the special function of the Anglo-Irish. Just at this time Yeats in the Irish Senate was to claim for the Anglo-Irish that they were no petty people, that they had created the most of the country's modern literature and the best of its political intelligence. He made that speech in the worst possible context—a debate on the undesirability of divorce in Ireland—and he offended many by his

[28] *Irish Statesman*, 19 Jan. 1924.
[29] S. O'Neill, in *Irish Statesman*, 2 Feb. 1924.
[30] *Irish Statesman*, 30 Aug. 1924.

intemperateness.[31] They were not to know that his arrogant pronouncement had more to do with a view of the eighteenth century he was then fashioning to underpin his doctrine of the aristocratic stance necessary to the artist in a demagogic age, than it had to do with current Irish realities. Yet AE, who was so much closer to those realities, often used the same litany of names— Berkeley, Swift, Burke, Goldsmith, to which he usually added those of George Moore, Synge, Lady Gregory, and Yeats himself. As he saw it, their crowning achievement was that they were the bridge which linked Irish culture with the wider world. Ireland, as he said over and over again, needed both. 'The cultural implications of the words Sinn Féin are evil. We are not enough for ourselves. No race is. All learn from each other. All give to each other. We must not be afraid of world thought or world science. They will give vitality to our own nationality. If we shut the door against their entrance we shall perish intellectually, just as if we shut the door against the Gaelic we shall perish nationally.'[32]

Essentially the same point was made in a different way by a younger Irish writer, Francis Hackett, whose experiences in America had convinced him that a colonial attitude of mind could linger on in a country long after political independence had been won. In the nineteenth century the Anglo-Irish mind, he suggested, had been in part colonial and there was a danger that this colonialism might persist in one form or other, indeed that it might be intensified under modern conditions which made cultural permeation so easy. But there was also a danger that Irish culture, by stressing the Gaelic element, would cut itself off from the rest of the world and lapse into parochialism. Yet these, he insisted, were false antitheses. Anglo-Irish culture need not be colonial; neither need Irish culture be parochial. In short, there need be no unbridgeable chasm between Anglo-Irish and Irish. What he called Anglo-Irish culture was also Irish, because it was the work of artists whose work arose out of their experience of

[31] F. S. L. Lyons, 'W. B. Yeats and the Public Life of Ireland', in *New Divinity*, vol. vii; no. 1 (summer 1976), pp. 6–25.
[32] *Irish Statesman*, 17 Jan. 1925.

Ireland and who conveyed that experience to the limits of their
capacity. So considered, 'there is no antithesis between Irish
culture and Anglo-Irish culture, between culture and the Catholic
Church ... between Ireland and Protestantism'. And this was so
because culture could only properly be considered in a nation's
relation to its creators, its writers, thinkers, and citizens who
expressed its spirit. The possession of a national language did not
ensure that this would happen, any more than the absence of a
national language would prevent it happening. The true antitheses
were between culture and colonialism, between culture and
parochialism. 'Parochialism will cripple Ireland unless Anglo-Irish
culture is enlisted against it.' Equally, 'the colonialism we detest
cannot be fought without the Anglo-Irish'.[33]

At bottom, this was the old argument for cultural fusion and,
as usual, it went unregarded save by the few who were already
converted. And so the debate continued year after year. Did it
have an end, and if so how and when? In a sense it has not ended
yet, and will never end so long as different cultures mingle and
collide in Ireland. But we can, perhaps, detect a turning-point in
the decade between 1928 and 1937. During that period the
sounds of battle gradually died down, not because the issue had
been resolved to anyone's satisfaction, but because the proponents
of one side of the argument had begun to droop and die. If we
look for a moment at the simple sequence of events we shall see a
perceptible movement in a particular direction. In 1928 Yeats
ceased to be a senator and in effect left public life. In 1929 the
Censorship of Publications Act was passed over the bitter
opposition of the Anglo-Irish and some others. In 1930 the *Irish
Statesman* ceased publication. In 1931 the Cork writer, Daniel
Corkery, published *Synge and Anglo-Irish Literature*, perhaps the
most sustained attack on the whole concept of Anglo-Irish
culture ever written;[34] true, it was immediately denounced by

---

[33] *Irish Statesman*, 21 Feb. 1925.

[34] Corkery seemed to be maintaining that only an Irish Catholic nationalist
could really write Irish literature, because only such a writer could do justice to
'the three great forces ... working for so long in the Irish Being'. Identifying
these as 'the religious consciousness of the people', Irish nationalism, and the land,
he regarded the Anglo-Irish as incapable of penetrating those mysteries.

writers who were not Anglo-Irish as totally false, and indeed as 'wrong-headed and damnable', but its influence in its day was considerable.[35] In 1932 there came to power Mr de Valera and his party, pledged to greater self-sufficiency and to the ideal of a Gaelic Ireland. In that same year also Lady Gregory died, and in Dublin the Eucharistic Congress exhibited to the world an Ireland which appeared to be wholly and devotedly Catholic. In 1933 imported newspapers were taxed. In 1935 the sale and importation of contraceptives was forbidden by law and the dance halls at last regulated to the satisfaction of the Roman Catholic hierarchy. And in that year AE, who had left Ireland the previous year, died in exile in Bournemouth. In 1937 the new constitution in a single document established a virtual republic in Ireland ('externally associated' with the Commonwealth since the previous year), restated the ultimate objective of a politically united Ireland, and brought together the Catholic social thinking of the past two decades.

The drift towards the Gaelic, Catholic concept of nationality seems unmistakable. Of the great figures of the renaissance the only one left to confront the flowing tide was Yeats, and Yeats in these last years, though reaching new heights as a poet, in public matters blew with an uncertain trumpet. More and more he seemed to be retreating from his early ideal of the fusion of cultures into an Anglo-Irish eighteenth century of his own fabrication—a creation which had little to do with history, but a great deal to do with his hungry quest for authority in the modern world.[36] That quest took him briefly into contact with

---

[35] Daniel Corkery, *Synge and Anglo-Irish Literature* (Cork, 1931). For the critical reaction, see especially the review by P. S. O'Hegarty in *Dublin Magazine*, vol. viii, no. 1 (new series, Jan.-Mar. 1932), pp. 51-6; and the longer essay 'Daniel Corkery', by S. O'Faoláin in *Dublin Magazine*, vol. xi, no. 2 (new series, Apr.-June 1936), pp. 49-61.

[36] It was true that with his creation of the Irish Academy of Letters in 1932 he did seem to be trying to bridge all possible chasms. The first group of academicians included some of the Anglo-Irish old guard, but also the new generation of southern Irish realists, a few northern Protestants, and even one or two expatriates including the most famous of them all—Bernard Shaw. However, the Academy was intended primarily as a defence of artistic freedom, rather than as a renewed attempt to fuse cultures.

an Irish version of European fascism in the early 1930s, but this was little to his liking. What he really wanted, he wrote in 1933, was 'the despotic rule of the educated classes', the triumph of the aristocratic principle over mass democracy. 'Do not,' he said in 1938, 'try to pour Ireland into any political system. Think first how many able men the country has, how many it can hope to have in the near future, and mould your system upon these men. It does not matter how you get them, but get them. Republics, Kingdoms, Senates, Corporate States, Parliaments, are trash, as Hugo said of something else, "not worth one blade of grass that God gives for the nest of the linnet".'[37]

Within a year Yeats was dead and there was a certain poetic justice in the fact that he should have died out of the country, for the country itself had been moving away from him for some years past. It had moved away, not merely from his proud defence of the Anglo-Irish virtues as he saw them, but also from AE's gentler insistence upon the need to reconcile the co-existing cultures. On the other hand, it could be said that in the twenty-six counties, at any rate, it was perhaps less urgent than it had been to campaign for a fusion of cultures, since this had at last begun to happen, not through legislation or conscious decision, but in the natural course of events. While the Anglo-Irish were quietly dying from the land a new generation of writers had emerged for whom it was no longer necessary to debate the rival merits of an Irish literature in English and an Irish literature in Irish. Bilingual themselves, even though writing mainly in English, men like Sean O'Faoláin, Frank O'Connor, and Brian O'Nolan moved easily and expertly from one to the other, demonstrating fusion in their own work. To those names should be added those of Peadar O'Donnell, Sean O'Casey, and Liam O'Flaherty. Each of these was unmistakably Irish and each, writing in English, contributed powerfully, like the three already mentioned, to a swing away from revolutionary romanticism towards deeply disenchanted realism. Another, very different figure, Francis Stuart, spoke for all of them when he wrote in one of his auto-biographical works of how Dublin had changed from 'a city full

[37] W. B. Yeats, *On the Boiler* (Dublin, 1939), p. 13.

of adventure and romance' into a place 'drab, respectable and dead'. 'And it was this spirit of smugness and deadness that we fought against and were defeated by. The spirit of liberal democracy. We fought to stop Ireland falling into the hands of publicans and shopkeepers and she had fallen into their hands.'[38]

Yet the flowering of post-revolutionary talent did not make for an easier life for the creative artist. On the contrary, all of these writers—and one might instance also among the poets Yeats's chief successors, Austin Clarke and Patrick Kavanagh—found themselves frequently in conflict with the restrictive and stifling society in which they had to work and from which, for a time at least, they sought to escape. O'Nolan, for example, a civil servant by profession, did his best work under pseudonyms— Flann O'Brien, Myles na Copaleen—and took refuge in satirical comment on the Ireland of his day, wittier and more scathing than anything that had been heard since Joyce. O'Connor and O'Faoláin would both have starved if they had had to rely on an Irish audience or on Irish publishers. As it was, they not only published in England and America, but for considerable periods earned their livelihoods in one or other of those countries. Sean O'Faoláin, it is true, stood his ground during the war years and in his periodical, *The Bell*, fought almost single-handed a running battle against the censorship, but the strain of this was too great, and the magazine ceased publication after fourteen years (1940– 54), during which it had opened the door to a whole new generation of writers.[39]

---

[38] Francis Stuart, *Things to Live For* (London, 1934), pp. 253–4. Stuart was born in Australia in 1902, spent his boyhood in county Antrim, was educated at Rugby, married (as his first wife) Maud Gonne's daughter Iseult, and fought on the republican side in the civil war. He moved for a time in Yeats's circle and was associated with him in launching *Tomorrow* in 1934, a periodical which affronted so many conventional pieties that it collapsed after a couple of issues. Until the Second World War (most of which he spent teaching literature in Berlin) Stuart lived mostly in Wicklow; he returned to Ireland in 1958 and published his most recent work in 1977. His writing, always intense, often brilliant, sometimes mannered, sets him apart from his contemporaries, but it has provided a valuable, if intermittent, link with the world of continental ideas not generally accessible to Irishmen in the generation after independence.

[39] See especially D. Foley, 'Monotonously Rings the Little Bell', and H.

It would not only be trite to say that what these writers were reacting against was Irish provincialism, it would also be inadequate. Of course, Ireland was provincial and had been for centuries. But the term needs to be defined. Provincialism in this instance does not mean remoteness from the seat of metropolitan culture and imprisonment in some local, inward-looking sub-culture. It means the very opposite, it means a turning towards the metropolitan—or, if you like, the cosmopolitan—and an abasement before the dominant culture which was still, as always, English. From that kind of provincialism some sought refuge in passionate attachment to place—what Patrick Kavanagh called 'parochialism' or John Hewitt, the Ulster poet, called 'regionalism'. But this, too, had its dangers. For the individual artist it might be the means of salvation, but for the society as a whole it could, and often did, mean introversion, a thickening of that obscurantism against which the writers themselves were protesting. The tension between the provincial and the parochial was not new. As we have seen, the whole Anglo-Irish drive towards fusion had been intended to create a culture which would avoid equally the extremes of abject servility to alien modes and complacent contemplation of native modes. All that had happened was that with the virtual disappearance of the Anglo-Irish, the new generation of writers, 'Irish' without the need of any qualifying label, had now to take up the double fight against cosmopolitanism without and insularity within.

On both fronts it was a hard fight. In Mr de Valera's Ireland the leading motifs were still Gaelicism and Catholicism. But whereas in the twenty-six counties Catholicism was all-pervasive, Gaelicism in any true sense seemed to be vanishing over the rim of the western horizon. That there was a deep psychological need to insist upon the primacy of Gaelic culture is easy to understand, but there can be no denying the conclusion that this insistence, at the moment when the claims of the revivalists seemed most to lack substance, introduced an element of unreality into modern Irish life. That unreality was heightened by a like attachment to

Butler, '*The Bell*: an Anglo-Irish view', in *Irish University Review*, vol. vi, no. 1, spring 1976, pp. 54–62 and 66–72.

another dogma, held with equal sincerity, but also contributing to the confusion and frustration of the time. This was the dogma of a united, or reunited, Ireland. In the south it was taken so much for granted as the ultimate object of policy that it was never a matter of party controversy, except perhaps on the ritual occasions when the opposition periodically berated the government for the slowness with which the always-to-be-desired, but never-to-be-actually-worked-for union was coming about. One reason why it did not come about was that few people in the Irish Free State seemed much interested in understanding either the structure or the ideology of Ulster unionism. Admittedly, if what we saw earlier of the intransigence of that unionism is any guide, understanding would not by itself have greatly helped the south towards a fusion which the north did not want at any price, but it might at least have allowed the two parts of Ireland to have a clearer view of each other.

However, that is not really the point. The point rather is that in the Irish Free State official thinking on partition continued to be based on the assumption that since Britain still occupied a portion of what the 1937 constitution termed 'the national territory', the first requirement was to end that occupation. The advantage of this somewhat simple-minded analysis for those who made it was that it staved off the necessity for coming to terms with the actualities of the northern situation. As any of the communities at grips with each other in that small province could have testified, support for partition was formidable, not because it was the last remnant of an outmoded colonialism, but because it was rooted in a variety of historical and contemporary circumstances which made the south abhorrent and an object of dark suspicion to the northern Protestant. The power of the Roman Catholic church in education, welfare, and society in general; the lingering influence of the civil war in the public life of the twenty-six counties and the ambiguous attitude of responsible politicians towards the I.R.A.; the restrictions on family life and on the freedom of the individual implied in the denial of divorce, the ban on contraception, and the operation of the *Ne Temere* decree which in effect dictated that the children of mixed marriages should be brought up as Catholics; the censorship of books (and, to a lesser extent, of films); the emphasis upon compulsory Irish—all this conveyed to the northern Protestant mind an overpowering impression of Catholicism, Gaelicism, and authoritarianism triumphant and triumphalist.

Although inevitable in the light of history, both recent and remote, this suspicious recoil was in its way just as simple-minded as the southern view of partition. It ignored too many facets of the complex whole. It ignored, for example, the extent to which the sundered parts of Ireland shared a common personality and a common past. By a curious irony it was during these very decades of division that in history, geography, anthropology, archaeology, and the study of folklore, scholars on both sides of the border were discovering and documenting what, quoting Professor Estyn Evans, I referred to in my first lecture as the 'essential unity' of Ireland. Moreover, the researches of these scholars were for the most part conducted under the auspices of learned societies which recognized no frontier. Neither, for that matter, did the Churches, or many businesses and professional bodies, to say nothing of sporting clubs and societies. It ought never to be forgotten that there has always been more friendly intercourse between the two parts of Ireland than extremists on either side have been willing to admit. Again, the northern view of the south as a totally alien community ignored certain basic facts—that in such matters as agricultural development, slum clearance, emigration, and unemployment, the problems of the Free State and of Northern Ireland were, up to 1939, broadly similar and evoked broadly similar solutions.

Most of all, northern exclusivism ignored the continued dominance on both sides of the border of the English culture or, more precisely, the emerging Anglo-American culture. The facile distinction between the progressive, industrial north-east and the rest of lazy, backward, rural Ireland underestimates the extent to which the whole island was being increasingly subjected to the pressures of the commercial civilization that held it in a pincer grip. Mass-produced commodities in the shops, newspapers and pulp magazines, books despite the censorship, films despite the censorship, the radio, the gramophone, emigrants' home thoughts from abroad, better, emigrants' home remittances from abroad, all of these drew all of Ireland inexorably towards the middle of the twentieth century. The process, it is true, was to be severely distorted by the Second World War which was so clearly a watershed in the history of intra-Irish relations. During those six years the south, locked into its neutrality, came perhaps nearer than ever before or since to Mr de Valera's ideal of a small God-fearing, Gaelic-orientated, mainly self-sufficient, mainly agricultural society. By contrast the north, for part of that time a crucial factor in the very survival of the United Kingdom, shared both the prosperity and the rising expectations of the new world that victory at last brought into precarious existence. It was no accident that in the arts and indeed in the general conduct of life, it was precisely at this time that a sense of a separate Ulster identity began to declare itself even in the midst of a still sharply divided society.

The mere fact that Northern Ireland had been established for a generation, that it had its own parliament, its own government, its own civil service, that it had to grapple with the problems of poverty and unemployment, and in doing so had to fight its corner within a United Kingdom that preferred to believe the Irish question had at last gone quietly away—all this had prepared the way for the emergence of that separate identity. Conditioned as we have become by later events to regard the whole history of the northern experiment in devolution as a history of communal friction, it is easy to overlook the fact that while northern Protestants and northern Catholics did not abandon their suspicions of each other, decade by decade and almost despite themselves they were being bound together within an entity which was recognizably different from either Britain or the Irish Free State.

In cultural matters, it is true, what historians of the arts in Northern Ireland have repeatedly called 'the time lag' between their province and the outside world was only gradually overcome. As late as 1951 the Ulster poet, John Hewitt, could still observe that since the gospel of material progress had possessed the province in the second half of the nineteenth century, 'poets in Ulster have . . . had to endure a climate of antagonistic opinion, and endeavour to establish a precarious foothold in a community, at worst self-righteous in its arrogant disavowal of the arts, at best ostentatiously indifferent to them'.[40] Yet even as he wrote the picture was changing. The drama, never by any means moribund, became livelier than ever during and after the war, with the creation of the Arts Theatre and of the Lyric Players' Theatre.[41] A new generation of painters grew to maturity, and though some of them lived wholly or intermittently elsewhere, the work of Daniel O'Neill, George Campbell, John Luke, Gerard Dillon, and Colin Middleton began to be better known in the province, especially after the establishment during the 1940s of a gallery in Belfast under the auspices of the Council for the Encouragement of Music and the Arts (now the Arts Council of Northern Ireland). And in poetry also new voices began to be heard—those of W. R. Rodgers, Robert Greacen, Roy McFadden, Maurice Craig, John Hewitt, and John Montague, for example—and though here too emigration took its toll, the time lag was ceasing to be the defence mechanism it once had been.[42]

These developments were important for two reasons. First, nearly all the writers and artists here mentioned addressed themselves to the northern scene and to northern themes, some more directly and successfully than others, but most of them with a clear consciousness that there was something true and significant to be said about the place that had bred them. And secondly, in their work the painters and poets and dramatists seemed almost nonchalantly to cross and recross the traditional cultural divides within the province. Yet perhaps that nonchalance was itself

[40] John Hewitt, 'Ancestral Voices: Sonnets by William Alexander (1824–1911), Archbishop of Armagh', *Rann*, no. 13 (1951), pp. 21–3; see also Hewitt's articles 'Writing in Ulster', in *The Bell*, vol. xviii (July 1952), pp. 197–202, and 'Poetry and Ulster: a survey', in *Poetry Ireland*, no. 8 (Jan. 1950), pp. 3–10.

[41] Sam Hanna Bell, *The Theatre in Ulster*, chaps. 6 and 7.

[42] Michael Longley (ed.), *Causeway: the Arts in Ulster* (Belfast and Dublin, 1971), *passim*. Since the above was written new light has been thrown on Ulster art, and on one painter in particular, by John Hewitt's affectionate and perceptive essay, *John Luke (1906–1975)*. This, published by the Arts Councils of Ireland in 1978 (and printed in Antrim), was evoked by an important exhibition of the artist's work, shown both in Belfast and in Trinity College, Dublin.

deceptive. The community of art existed, or at any rate was struggling to be born, but it could not obliterate the enmities which separated one culture from another. Out of those enmities, indeed, would come a new efflorescence—especially of poetry in the work of such as Seamus Heaney, Michael Longley, Derek Mahon, and Patrick Muldoon—but so too would come an eruption of violence so dire and so prolonged as to bring home at last to an astonished world the force of the volcanic fires that still burned beneath the unquiet surface of Ulster life.

It would be quite wrong, therefore, to end these lectures either by dwelling unduly upon the 'essential unity' of Ireland or upon the exposure of both of its parts to Anglo-American pressures. But it would be equally wrong to ascribe the diverging fortunes and attitudes of north and south simply to the Second World War, important as its effects undoubtedly were. It has been my principal purpose to establish a longer perspective and to lay beside the essential unity of Ireland a no less essential diversity. That diversity, as I have sought to show, has been a diversity of ways of life which are deeply embedded in the past and of which the much-advertised political differences are but the outward and visible sign. This was the true anarchy that beset the country. During the period from the fall of Parnell to the death of Yeats, it was not primarily an anarchy of violence in the streets, of contempt for law and order such as to make the island, or any part of it, permanently ungovernable. It was rather an anarchy in the mind and in the heart, an anarchy which forbade not just unity of territories, but also 'unity of being', an anarchy that sprang from the collision within a small and intimate island of seemingly irreconcilable cultures, unable to live together or to live apart, caught inextricably in the web of their tragic history.

> Out of Ireland have we come;
> Great hatred, little room,
> Maimed us at the start.

INDEX